"Dr. Johnson's timely contribution to the lay literature years, their attendant losses and need for caregiver companionship is aimed at a wide audience, appropriately so. As a retired physician with well over 40 years of experience, I highly recommend her book to family, as well as institutional caregivers, nursing home and assisted living staff and anyone who is a member of the 'aging' populace."

Jacob W. Cambier, M.D. – Oregon.

"A must read! In Dr. Johnson's 'A Caregiver's Guide: Insights into the Later Years,' she shows she understands the heart of a caregiver and the issues that we face as a society eager to understand and have the tools to become the greatest generation of caregivers. Because of her journey, we now have this wonderful guide for all caregivers to learn from, embrace, and share with anyone who is caring for another. Caring for someone you love is a gift and caring for yourself is the gift you can give yourself by understanding and reading what Dr. Johnson is sharing with her readers."

Rick Cseak, CSA (Certified Senior Advisor), Owner/CEO of Home Helpers Senior Care at Home – Colorado.

"What a comprehensive and engaging guide for professional and family caregivers alike! *A Caregiver's Guide: Insight into the Later Years* provides information that is beneficial through every step of the caregiving relationship. The author presents the information in a thoughtful and compassionate style, which puts the reader at ease. As a Professional Geriatric Care Manager, I highly recommend this valuable compilation of knowledge, derived from the author's personal and professional experiences."

Mary Galvez, MA, CMC (Care Manager Certified), NCG (National Certified Guardian), Owner of Guardianship and Care Management Services, LLC – New Mexico.

"Dr. Johnson has written a truly wonderful and infinitely helpful guide, taking the reader into and through the complexities of aging, loss, and grief, in comprehensive, engaging, clear, and poignant ways. Her evocative vignettes, both personal and clinical, on difficult-to-face topics, are exquisite and enlightening. She raises issues that we think of asking about, but shy away from. She answers our questions before they even have a chance to rise to our lips. Dr. Johnson beautifully weaves personal experience through professional knowledge and expertise, in touching, powerful, and sometimes humorous ways. As an internist/psychiatrist/psychotherapist who teaches self-care, I deeply appreciate Mary Johnson's keen awareness and articulation of the mind/emotion-body-spirit connection. Thank you, Dr. Johnson, for giving us an up-close-and-personal/professional look at how real life unfolds. Every one of us needs this important resource at our side."

Storme Lynn, M.D. – New Mexico.

"Mary Johnson is exceptionally good at what she does and, consequently, has written an excellent resource guide for those who also want to excel at caring for the elderly – whether a loved one, a friend, or a resident in a retirement community. The information provided is easy to read, understand, and to put into practice. This is a 'must read' for anyone who loves and/or cares for a senior!"

Linda R. McGrath, RCFE
(Residential Care Facilitator for Elderly),
Former Sales & Marketing Executive, Senior Housing Industry – Idaho.

"Heartfelt caregiver guide sprinkled with real life experience and topped with compassionate advice! Reading this wonderful book led me to reflect on many of my own experiences. The words of wisdom let me know that I was on the right path in supporting my parents as they age and deal with different health issues. Dr. Johnson shines such a warm light on the need to take into account the losses people experience as they go through life. Sharing her personal stories throughout made the information so much more real! There are many resources available, but this one is so personal it touches the reader in a way that is informative and comforting at the same time. We are all on our own caregiving journey. The road is often long and rocky. This is the perfect guide to take with you as you travel that road!"

Mary G. Martinez, CEO, Gerontologist,
Franchise Owner of Home Instead Senior Care – New Mexico.

"Much of Dr. Mary Johnson's knowledge on this subject is based on her personal experiences as a caregiver, manager of care facilities, educator, and counselor. Caregivers will feel her compassion and warmth on how to address grief issues as they read through these pages. This book should be required reading not only for caregivers, but for geriatric students as well as geriatric physicians."

Irene Ter Haar, R.N., LNHA
(Licensed Nursing Home Administrator),
QMRP (Qualified Mental Retardation Professional),
Retired State Surveyor/Inspector of Long-term
Healthcare Facilities – Iowa.

A Caregiver's Guide: Insights into the Later Years

A Caregiver's Guide: Insights into the Later Years

Mary A. Johnson Ph.D.

PMJ Associates, Inc. Press
Albuquerque, NM, USA
2015

www.maryajohnsonphd.com
www.pmjassociatesincpress.com

ISBN 9780996202909
ISBN: 0996202900
Library of Congress Control Number: 2015905296
Mary A. Johnson, Ph.D., Pendleton, OR

PMJ Associates, Inc. Press
Albuquerque, NM, USA

Dedicated to
Zoe Louise Wright Anderson
and Paul Tefteller Johnson,
both of whom I had the privilege of attending during the final years
of
their lives
and
both of whom taught me a great deal of all I know about life,
growing older, and life's end.

Table of Contents

Foreword

I FIRST MET MARY JOHNSON in the 1970's, when she was a student in a magazine writing class I was teaching at the University of New Mexico. She was slightly older than the average student and had the seriousness and focus that are marks of maturity. But it wasn't until she turned in her finished article that I realized what lay behind the depth I sensed in this woman. She already had lived through a tragedy that the typical starry-eyed college kids could never have dreamed of. Her first person article, "Cathy Goes Home," was about the unexpected death of her 4-year-old daughter and the effort it took her to step past her own grief in order to provide strength and comfort to the rest of her family.

I was the mother of five, and could not conceive of anything more unbearable. Tears streamed down my face as I read her story—not just for the content, but for the woman who had the courage to write it.

To get an A in my class, a student had to sell an article to a national magazine. Mary easily got that A.

Since then, she has utilized that same compassion in her choice of careers. She earned her Ph.D. in a branch of psychology and worked in the healthcare field, both as a grief counselor and as an employee of several nursing homes, and manager of a retirement apartment complex and several assisted living facilities. Her knowledge in this area was painfully honed by her personal life as she served as caregiver, first for elderly parents and then for a husband afflicted with leukemia.

When Mary told me of her desire to write a guide book for caregivers, I was strongly supportive of the project, since by that time tragedy had struck my own life. At age 18, the youngest of my own children had been chased down in her car and shot twice in the head by unidentified gunmen. The doctor informed us that, if Kait survived, it would be as little more than a vegetable. Faced with the possibility that I would spend the rest of my days taking care of my daughter's deteriorating body, an empty shell with the kernel of awareness removed from it, I was overwhelmed not only by grief but by impotence. How would I know what to do and, more importantly, find the strength to do it?

Kait did me the kindness of passing away in the hospital. But that nightmare event caused me to realize how abruptly fate can turn on us and how unprepared most of us are to deal with the responsibilities that may be required of us when that occurs.

Of course, our own daughter's situation was comparatively rare. However, it is inevitable that at one point in our lives the majority of us—primarily women—are going to have to become caregivers to people we love who have reached a point at which they no longer can care for themselves. The very fact that science has extended the average lifetime far beyond what was once thought possible has opened the gate to problems that are unavoidable for an aging population—feebleness, the loss of control of bodily functions, various forms of dementia, and mounting depression as loss piles upon loss – loss of strength and energy, of productive careers that often defined the person's identity, of physical beauty, of mobility, of a social life, and perhaps most important, of personal dignity.

A Caregiver's Guide: Insights into the Later Years is an outstanding guide book, not only for caregivers, but also for aging people who need help in understanding and accepting their changing situation. The information is educational, valuable, and useful, and the points are illustrated by true case histories based upon the author's own experiences. Other books have been written on this topic, but few from the viewpoint of an excellent writer who is both a respected professional in the field of eldercare and a mother-daughter-wife who has cared for her own loved ones during their final years and helped them leave this world as painlessly and peacefully as possible.

I was proud to be asked to write a foreword for this book. I think it's important for the general population to read it, even if the subject is not one that they are currently dealing with. In fact, I plan to send a copy to each of my four surviving children to help them prepare for the day when they may find themselves responsible for either providing or arranging for the care of their father and me.

– Lois Duncan

Lois Duncan is the award-winning author of over 50 books besides her most recent, *One to the Wolves: On the Trail of a Killer*, about the search for her daughter's murderer. Her works include children's books, books of poetry, many young adult novels, and adult nonfiction books. Among them: *Who Killed My Daughter?; How to Write and Sell Your Personal Experiences; Down a Dark Hall; Stranger with My Face; I Know What You Did Last Summer*; and the movie box office hit, *Hotel for Dogs.*

Introduction

I FIRST MET DR. MARY Johnson when she invited me to be on her dissertation committee. I was intrigued with her ideas on aging; the last stages of life were in accord with the research I was reading regarding the first stages of life. Since I knew she would enliven my synthesizing of the research, of the new-at-the-time ideas that infants were not blank slates waiting to be written on but alert, open creatures reaching for connection from the very beginning, I agreed.

No matter where in the continuum of life we are, we hunger for connection. Dr. Johnson and I both agreed that the human spirit demands that we be seen, heard, understood, and valued. We agreed that this connection is our life blood and without it we wither away. Without attention and understanding we become dry, desiccated and lonely because we find ourselves through others.

Dr. Johnson's dissertation was designed to find a way to alleviate the despair and anger of many of her older patients. She was able to show that writing the incidents of their lives, even if they were painful, and putting them in some meaningful order, within an understanding of the motives behind the behavior, gave the elderly an opportunity to assess their lives with a deeper acknowledgment of what had moved them and a kinder assessment of who they were. The narrative helped reassure, but the joy came from sharing these insights with family and friends.

Dr. Johnson has maintained her interest in interaction with others as the main ingredient in ameliorating anxiety over aging. She intends to share her understanding of the major ingredients of unhappy aging with the caregivers of the elderly – family and friends – and what the remediation for this unhappiness requires. She has come to the conclusion that the roots of depression and acting out in the elderly are based on unresolved grief. It is a lack of connection with another over loss. She delineates many losses that go ungrieved because of a deprivation of understanding over the meaning of loss, by the self and others, and of the elements of loss and grief. This book is a reminder of the consequences of loss to our sense of self. It is a compendium of losses we often disregard. It is meant to remind us of the impact of all loss – big and inconsequential (and who is to say which is which?). This book is also a primer for what to look for, what to do, and how to help the elderly and oneself.

Dr. Johnson is writing about two different kinds of unresolved grief. One kind of unresolved grief is that of the past: lost loved ones, lost jobs or opportunities, lost material goods, lost value systems, lost ideals, lost hopes and dreams, lost beliefs. The other unresolved grief is that of the present: we are aging and we are losing our old "markers" of who we were. Both types of loss can be diminished, undervalued and put aside. Both types of loss can be unresolved and cause untold damage to our sense of integrity and pride.

The first group of unexpressed losses of the past need to be revisited. Sharing the narratives of one's life in the presence of an invested listener helps the elder truly grieve the unexpressed losses of that past time. Recognizing that many of these separations from others have been hallmarks in a life helps reassess one's past choices. For those whose mothers died in childbirth there is a deep, abiding sense of loss, never truly understood. Others lose a fetal twin and find they are always looking for someone, something they never could find. Recognizing the importance of this or any early life loss, often not explicitly remembered, helps one to actually grief the impact that loss had on their lives: the loss was physically felt and emotionally carried throughout their lives hidden from consciousness, but not from the feelings. We forget the name of the boy who didn't ask us to the prom, but we never lose the sensation of hurt we felt then. If we were too embarrassed to cry then, to share with a loving other, our mortification, our grief, it haunts us in old age. The loss is never grieved because it is not recognized as a loss.

There are many such unrecognized or discounted losses: you are reassured by others that the loss is nothing to worry about, is trivial, the object you lost can easily be replaced, it was just a thing, or the person who died "had a good life" or a long life; the physiological shock to your system is absolutely ignored. That shock, however, is registered in your implicit memory and contrives to exist without the remediation of shared re-structuring of the *new* you. New because loss changes you. Without another to share your pain the unresolved grief remains closeted in your psyche; you do not recognize you are a new person with new information about life.

Dr. Johnson's thesis is that the inability to cope with the reality of an aging self with grace comes from these unresolved griefs. This speaks directly to the unresolved emotional memory that still arises with all its original intensity, but which, when we are older, we are less capable of defending – holding at bay the hidden memory. If we're never able to express freely our thoughts and feelings to another who understands, we have never truly had the integration of all our selves: the joyous and sad selves, the prideful and shame filled selves – we have lived in compartments moving from one to other but never recognizing each place as part of our total self.

Dr. Johnson delineates primary losses from secondary and disenfranchised losses; the thesis, however, remains the same. Recognition of these losses, understanding of their significance and active, deliberate sharing of the thoughts and feeling over these losses will not only alleviate the lack of resolution but will indeed help the griever integrate pieces of lost selves.

The second group of losses, those of aging itself, are often disenfranchised. Aging, even for those who have had the good fortune to have loving kindness manifest in their lives, is not easy. The loss of our primary selves, our ability to function easily, to make decisions for ourselves, to have choices and independence, to be able to act on our own accord, perhaps the loss of financial stability are all at risk as we age.

Even for those who have somehow managed to salvage their sense of worth and purpose in life, find aging often robs them of the long held definition of who they are. We no longer look the same, we no longer move the same, we no longer think the same. Our senses betray us - the taste of food, the distant panorama, or the violin concert are no longer quite as clearly and profoundly experienced. We often don't seem able to perform sexually, even if we want to – and we even miss the desire to want to. If we have not already, we lose loved ones and friends and lose the joy of reminiscing and laughing in the comfort of really being known. It is a loss of all we have known of our selves.

We are forced by the process of aging to slowly give up parts of who we are - and though we know how much we have lost of our old self we often find no one with whom to communicate. "This old body doesn't look or act like me – what you see is not really who I am – I'm that younger, more confident, more competent person I was once. Can you see that person?" No? I am rushed with shame. As we age we begin to lose the sharp acuity of our explicit memory - nouns especially disappear. We wonder, "Are we losing our minds?" At the same time we maintain a high level of emotional memory.

Even the kindness and courtesy of others can be experienced as humiliation: one has lost agency over one's life and is dependent on others; one must adjust to caregivers' ways to accommodate the new inabilities. This is mortifying to those who have prided themselves on their independence. The emotions of shame and fear arise as one experiences loss of options, loss of freedom.

What is the essence of aging? It is loss and, finally, the recognition of loss of one's own life on this earth. We can modify the fear and grief by finding the *meaning* of our life and purpose in the remainder of our days. Dr. Johnson's goal is to offer elders and caregivers a guide to finding meaning. When we are able to do this we can give to the world our wisdom, joy and gratefulness. The last stage of our lives will either be regenerative or stagnant. Dr. Johnson in this new book is addressing why some people move into stagnation, depression, or acting out, rather than the serenity of a life understood and accepted.

Dr. Johnson is clear: *Expressing is resolving.* Most of resolving grief is sharing the emotions and thoughts we have had over our losses. The "I - thou" interchange between two people is the most important ingredient in healing. The brain changes to accommodate the new person you have become because of your loss. There is no escape from the change in you - but in order to truly understand that change, you need to express the pain and fear to another who can "hold" that grief, help you experience it, and greet the new you.

Dr. Johnson's premise is that if the caregiver and the elder understand the deeper emotions motivating their lives, the more graceful and fruitful will be the remainder of their lives. As elders reprise their journey with understanding they can give to those who travel with them, caring for them. This book was written for the caregivers of the aging – family members or professionals; but as Dr. Johnson suggests throughout, the lessons learned from infant and aging research are applicable to all of us throughout our lives. Vulnerability, emotional openness, to another is resolution of loss, and that resolution enables integrity and graceful acceptance.

Dr. Johnson interacts with her reader in an intimate and vulnerable way. Her book is in some ways a memoir of her life and losses; her style is colloquial and inviting. She is modeling exactly what she recommends caregivers do with their older charges. This leaves the reader believing in the verity and wisdom of which she speaks.

– *Marythelma Brainard, Ph.D.*
Psychologist in Private Practice
Albuquerque, New Mexico

Preface

I HOPE THIS BOOK MAY make caregiving easier for family caregivers and for professional caregivers, either in patients' homes or in nursing homes, assisted living communities, and senior apartment complexes. The more you know, the better you can cope. If you don't understand how things affect you and others, you have no way of working out a coping strategy.

I have observed many elderly people during the years I worked in nursing homes, obtained a nursing home administrator's license, and managed a retirement apartment complex and assisted living communities. I eventually became licensed as a counselor and went into private practice, specializing in grief and loss.

As I counseled the elderly, I realized that many, if not most, of their reasons for coming to counseling (or in some cases, being *sent* to counseling) had roots in unexpressed grief of many, many kinds. Some families and caregivers were frustrated with the older people's depression and acting-out behavior, and couldn't understand why they continued to be depressed or exhibited inappropriate behavior, when they had good homes and loving care. As I began to ask about losses in the older people's lives, they would open up to me about the things that had changed, losses they had experienced, and the disappointments they felt.

Both men and women experience losses. I find the "he/she" combination cumbersome both to write and to read; therefore, the gender pronouns used will sometimes be "he" and sometimes "she," and except for gender-specific topics, will be interchangeable. Also, to eliminate confusion, the word "patient" will be used throughout the book to denote the person being cared for.

This book deals with the losses that many times occur as we age, although the principles can apply to people of any age. In a talk I gave recently, one younger woman in a wheelchair spoke up and said, "What you're saying can as easily apply to disabled people as to the elderly. We go through many of the same losses." She was right, of course. I can see the similarity of the situations. Perhaps this book will appeal to younger disabled people, their families, and their caregivers for that reason.

However, it is primarily written to help families understand the losses and grief of the elderly, and help professional or family caregivers understand and work successfully with elderly patients. It can also help the elderly themselves acknowledge their losses and begin to process them, resolve them, and move forward in life. In Harden's book, *Voices of Wisdom: Hawaiian Elders Speak*, John Keola Lake, a respected Hawaiian teacher and a renowned chanter says wisely, "We have to mend the past so that we can move into the future."

Elderly people experience many losses over a lifetime. We will look at changes in appearance, changes in health, and the loss of loved ones, as well as many other changes that impact the lives of the elderly, their families, and their caregivers. Examining these issues will provide better understanding of the grief process that occurs in many older people and affects their moods and behaviors.

Understanding is the first step toward facing reality and learning to cope with change and loss. When these changes and losses are better understood, and ways of dealing with the feelings of loss are practiced, elderly patients, their families, and caregivers may interact with less anxiety and depression.

How do we define "elderly?" The U.S. Department of Housing and Urban Development (HUD) defines elderly as being at least 62 years of age. The AARP requirement for membership is now age 50, and most "senior discounts" apply to individuals 55, 60, 62, or 65 years old. Academics in the aging field generally refer to groups of aging people as the "young old," the "old," and the "old old." Age categories vary, but often the young old are 65-74, the old are 75-84, and the old old are 85 and over. Some older people take issue with being categorized in this way.

It is easy to see that no one can define "elderly" with any degree of agreement. I prefer the generally accepted usage as referring to persons in later life. Whatever later life is can be left up to the reader. When we are teens, we think of people in their 30s as being in later life, but as we age, we move the definition of later life back farther and farther, until we see people in their 80s not wanting to live in retirement communities with others they call old. My mother-in-law, who was 81, had to live for a while in an assisted living community, and she complained to us that she didn't want to live with "all those old folks." Let's just leave the definition as "people who are aging," and that includes all of us, especially those of us past mid-life.

We will look at losses many people experience as they grow older. Losses can be thought of as primary losses, or those that occur initially, and secondary losses, or those that occur as a result of some primary loss. The secondary losses are often overlooked by society. There are also "disenfranchised losses," those that carry some kind of stigma and are not given the social support the grievers want and need. Often it is difficult to categorize a loss, and as you will see, they are so intertwined in many lives that it may be helpful to see them as a circle of losses rather than losses that are sequential. Since our discussion must of necessity be sequential, as the pages in a book, we will look first at an overview of the grief process, then primary losses, then at the secondary losses that often result. Later chapters address some special aspects of grief and suggest ways families and caregivers can help the elderly cope with their grief, process it, and move on to an enjoyable life.

One chapter deals with issues surrounding dementia, including Alzheimer's disease. Dementia is an umbrella term denoting a decline in memory and thinking processes, and Alzheimer's disease is but one form of dementia. It is a condition affecting many among our aging population. It is one of the most frustrating conditions for both the ones suffering from dementia and for their caregivers and requires special skills that families and caregivers can learn and adapt to their own situation to make caregiving less stressful.

There is a chapter about caregivers' needing to take good care of themselves, because we can't give more than we have, and if caregivers allow themselves to be depleted, they have to replenish their reserves in order to be effective caregivers. Learning about patients for whom you are given the opportunity to be caregivers is one phase of the job, the caregiving is the actual hands-on part, but taking care of yourselves is also a very important part. I stress this aspect now, at the beginning of the book, and again in a later chapter, because patients who *receive* the care deserve the very best you have to give, but you who *give* the care often appear in my office completely depleted, having given everything without taking measures to fill your reservoir again.

The last chapter looks at the dying process. Caring for the elderly will inevitably include the death of a person or persons. Caring for a dying person requires certain knowledge and skills.

This book is intended to give you greater understanding of your patients and allow you to have a more meaningful caregiving experience. You have a tremendous opportunity not only to serve the needs of your patients, but to do it with an extra element of enjoyment!

–The author

CHAPTER 1

Understanding Grief

ALTHOUGH MANY PEOPLE USE THE terms "bereavement" and "grief" interchangeably, there is a difference. When we look at the roots of each word, we begin to see the meanings in a different way.

The word "bereavement" developed from a variety of words from early languages, all meaning "to take away by violence," "to deprive ruthlessly or by force," or "to deprive or make desolate," especially by death. Thus, we have bereavement as the state of having had something taken away by force, of having been robbed or plundered. When we have the life of someone we hold dear taken away against our will, we do indeed feel robbed.

However, when anything dear to us is taken away against our will or of necessity, the same kinds of feelings result, although not usually to the degree prompted by a death. Ask anyone whose home, apartment, room, or car has been burglarized, their possessions plundered, and some of those treasured items taken away.

Grief is our reaction to bereavement. When something is taken away against our will, we respond with grief. It is defined as keen mental suffering or distress over affliction or loss; sharp sorrow; or painful regret. The origins of the word are Middle English and Latin words meaning "heavy" and "to burden." Thus, when we respond to bereavement, we suffer distress, sorrow, and regret, and the grief feels as if we are carrying a heavy burden.

Have you ever noticed how people walk when they are grieving? Many times the shoulders are bent, and the posture is slightly slumped, as if they are carrying something heavy. Grief can seem very heavy, can weigh us down. Walk is slower, movement is labored. One client told me she feels as if she is "walking through knee-high mud, getting nowhere, and getting there very slowly."

We usually think of bereavement as denoting the death of a person, but it can also mean being deprived of anything we care deeply about. When we lose something precious, grief is our response. Think of a child who loses his favorite toy or blanket – the response is intense grief in the form of crying, sometimes physical action, as in the movement of arms and legs, then usually being difficult to distract, not wanting to do anything until the lost item is found.

My grandson left his favorite blanket, with which he had slept from the time he was born, on a plane as his family traveled to visit me. When he and his mother and sister deplaned and he and his mother realized his blanket was not with him, they were already in the baggage claim area. He asked for his "bankie," only to find it was not with them. He was inconsolable. The plane had already taken off with another load of passengers, and the loved blanket could not be retrieved. After we drove to my house from the airport, I dug into my closet, and among the older baby things I found a small, soft blanket similar in color to the one that had been lost. When it was offered to him, he would not accept it – "I want MY bankie!" His bereavement was the loss of his favorite blanket, and he had to grieve intensely for a while, crying and flailing his arms and legs as he lay on the floor. He finally fell asleep, exhausted from the episode.

In a day or two, he grudgingly took the "new" blanket, but he still had a hard time going to sleep at night without the loved one. As we study the grief response, we will see how many situations in life result in varying degrees of grief.

Think of the teen-age girl who looks forward to going to her senior prom, but when that event draws near, she has not been asked for a date. She may go anyway, and now going solo is more and more the custom among high schoolers who don't have dates, but the grief of not having been invited by someone as his or her date can be devastating.

I remember a good friend many years ago had looked forward all her high school years to that one special occasion, and she had dreamed of the boy with whom she wanted to go. Two weeks before the prom, she learned he had asked another classmate. She felt her life was ruined. Yes, teenagers can be dramatic, but it is grief nevertheless. The expectation, and then denial, of a lovely evening became for her a lifelong grief, one that could never be remedied, because there is only one senior prom in a lifetime. In her later life, as she lay very ill, we spoke of our high school days and laughed at most of the antics of those days. However, she brought up that prom, and the remembrance of the disappointment she had experienced still brought tears to her eyes.

Bereavement, or the loss of things dear to us, happens throughout our lives. We suffer losses of all kinds, but we rarely think of our responses to some of those losses as grief. We lose jobs, we lose possessions, we lose relationships, and many other things, and most people feel they should be strong and neither acknowledge nor give in to their feelings. As a result, many people are moving about their days carrying a heavy burden of grief and wondering why they can't move forward, or why they are depressed and lack motivation, or why they can't get along with other people. When clients come to me because they feel "stuck" in life, I begin to probe into their experiences with loss.

One of my colleagues, Dr. Marythelma Brainard, has studied the behavior of infants in the womb (Personal communication, Dr. Marythelma Brainard, April, 2013). She has found that infants who are deprived of their biological mother's care after birth, because of the mother's illness, death, or absence for other reasons, or because of adoption, suffer an experience similar to grief. They have spent about five months hearing the voice of the biological mother with its unique tone and cadence, hearing her heartbeat, and hearing the rush of her blood through her body. (A baby's hearing develops about the fourth month.) If all our experiences are recorded somewhere in the brain, as demonstrated by Dr. Willard Penfield in the 1950s, and reported by both reviewer J. A. Speyrer and author T. A. Harris, then somewhere is recorded the experience in the womb. Dr. Brainard says Freud's theory of an "oceanic feeling" has been interpreted by some as a desire to return to the blissful, euphoric feelings of floating in the womb.

When an infant begins, at birth, to hear the voice of another person, no longer the familiar voice to which the infant has become accustomed while in the womb, it is theorized the infant experiences a kind of grief for the familiar sounds. A sound machine that plays a recording of a human heartbeat can sometimes provide some continuity, even though each heartbeat is different, and a machine cannot exactly duplicate the infant's mother's heartbeat.

Eventually the infant becomes accustomed to the new voice, particularly if it is soothing, but Dr. Brainard believes remnants of this grief extend into adulthood. If so, elderly people who spent their early life being raised by someone other than their biological mother may still be carrying a subtle life-long grief that has never been recognized nor expressed.

Dr. Brainard believes other losses throughout life are influenced and compounded by this early and somewhat "hidden" grief. She says, "It is an imperfect memory of loss in the person forever. Christopher Bollas says some early experiences result in 'the unthought known,' meaning the imprint is physical (pre-thought) and beyond consciousness. By drawing on some theories of early experience, we begin to see the possibly very, very early beginnings of grief for some elders."

I have included this discussion of some of the roots of very early grief, because it may well have a bearing on some people's grief responses later in life. If, as Dr. Brainard says, this early grief is compounded by later life griefs, it is at least worth mentioning. Perhaps having a grieving patient share whether she was raised by someone other than her biological mother might open the door for a caregiver to receive and respond with understanding to this information, thereby validating some deep-seated longing that has been with the patient for life, but which has been unrecognized. Care must be taken not to play the role of therapist, but simply to be understanding and perhaps mention the theories that exist about experiences in the womb.

Even though there can be many losses during a lifetime, the grief response to the death of a loved one, be it family or friend, is often the deepest. We will look at that immense loss later in another chapter.

As we look at the many and varied losses the elderly have experienced and are experiencing, we begin to see more clearly the magnitude of their grief. Transitions after losses are often difficult, and loss upon loss intensifies the difficulty. Author MJ Harden tells of Jo-Anne Sterling, an artist who creates works of art with feathers and who says, "We somewhat live yesterday in combination with today."

In Chapter 2, we look at the primary losses. Primary losses are those that precipitate a cascade of secondary losses, and these secondary losses will be discussed in Chapter 3.

CHAPTER 2

Understanding the Primary Losses

Physical Changes

Changes in Appearance

As the body ages, its appearance changes in many ways. Some people cope with these changes matter-of-factly, some try to combat the visible signs of aging with various means of "camouflage" such as hair color, wigs, hair transplants, new hair styles to cover the hearing aids, wrinkle creams, clothing designed for a younger body, and processes that make wearing eyeglasses unnecessary.

In a recent issue of a national newspaper supplement, one article was titled "Take Years Off Your Looks – Instantly!" Another magazine, aimed at those over 50, has an advertisement that refers to the product advertised as "your own personal fountain of youth." At some point, many of us cease looking for the "fountain of youth" and begin adjusting to our aging. For some, it is not an easy adjustment and represents a grave (no pun intended) loss.

For people to whom appearance is a source of pride, the following changes represent tremendous loss. Some have said that by the time we're old, we are different people physically. For a comparison, look at the wedding anniversary section of any large metropolitan newspaper, and look for the couples married 50 or more years. Many times there is a wedding picture alongside their current picture, and even though the facial features of the current picture resemble those in the wedding picture, in almost all of them there are dramatic changes in appearance. For a more personal comparison, look at your own picture at age 15 or younger, then look into a mirror.

Hair

Some people inherit genes for prematurely gray hair that cause graying in their late teens or early 20s or 30s. For most of us, the first gray hairs appear sometime during our 40s or 50s. I remember my mother, a redhead, plucking out her first few gray hairs with tweezers, after finding them while looking into a magnifying mirror. Of course, it was a losing battle. People with red hair tend to gray more slowly, but even they eventually notice more gray than red. Some people attempt to camouflage the gray with commercial hair color. Some of you will remember the old Clairol ads, "Does she or doesn't she? Only her hairdresser knows for sure." Again, it may be a futile attempt, as sometimes gray hairs are not as receptive to a coloring agent, because when hairs have lost their pigment they also lose some ability to react to the dye. Some people, instead of choosing a color that complements their aging skin tone, try to duplicate the hair color they had when they were young, producing a ghastly unrealistic effect that only emphasizes to others they have dyed their hair in an attempt to cover the gray.

Some people, especially men, inherit genes for baldness and begin to lose hair as they age. This "male pattern baldness," as it is called, provides a fertile market for hair transplants, for toupees, and for various brands of chemical compounds that promote (or promise to promote) hair growth.

One of my first counseling offices was in the same building with a physician who did hair transplants. Most of the clientele were men who were just beginning to experience some hair loss at the crown. As they left the physician's office after a transplant, they appeared to be uncomfortable, so it must have been very important to them to regain hair.

Unless a toupee is well-matched to the real hair, well styled, and is attached so that it won't come loose easily, it can be almost comical. In a college I attended, a professor wore a toupee that had none of the above qualities except the comical appearance. It was all we students could do to keep straight faces in his classes. We were much younger, of course.

Women whose hair begins to thin often invest in wigs. A well-fitted and styled wig can appear very natural. These are usually sold in wig salons, and if the client requests, great care is taken to match the real hair and the normal style of the client. Less expensive wigs, sometimes ordered by mail or online, sometimes neither fit as well nor look as natural.

A portion of the wig business is for cancer patients who lose their hair, or for brain surgery patients whose hair has been shaved. These circumstances are different from the natural aging process. These patients use wigs to repair situations that are not due to normal aging, but which nonetheless represent losses to them.

I mention this because of three memories I have. One is of a young woman at a church I attended years ago. I passed her in the hall of the church building, and her hair was beautiful. I complimented her on the style, which was very becoming. She leaned over close to me and thanked me, but said quietly, "I am taking chemo and have lost my hair. This is a wig."

A second memory is of a young employee at a nursing home. She had a condition known as *alopecia areata*, which causes the loss of large areas of hair and can be of concern, especially to women. Wearing a wig was her way of coping with this situation.

Another memory is of my mother, who had brain surgery at age 87. Her head had to be shaved, and the doctor said when the stitches were out Mother would be able to wear a wig. Before the stitches were out, I went to a wig salon, taking with me photos of Mother taken before her surgery and a sample of her hair. The stylist matched her real hair and her hair style, and when the stitches came out and the wig could be worn, Mother looked very much like her former self.

While these are health-related examples, and therefore understandable reasons for women to don wigs, often wigs are worn because people aren't happy with their hair as they age naturally, and they try various means of "correcting" or enhancing nature.

Skin

Wrinkles form in once-smooth facial skin. Facial wrinkles and the motivation to erase them provide customers for many cosmetics that are supposed to eliminate wrinkles or for procedures such as injections of botulinum toxin, produced under several brand names. Some people are even willing to undergo surgery to tighten sagging facial or neck skin.

Skin texture on other parts of the body changes and becomes filled with tiny wrinkles. As the skin thins during aging, veins stand out. We may look at our hands and say, "These can't be my hands. Look how wrinkled they are!" My mother said, "I didn't realize I was getting older until I looked down and saw that my hands looked like my mother's hands."

Once when I was reading my granddaughter a book, she said, "Grammaw, why do your arms look like that?" She was pointing to the wrinkles that appear when my forearm is turned to hold a book. I had not noticed them until she called my attention to them, but there was no denying the tiny wrinkles that were there. I said, "I hadn't noticed them, but the wrinkles must be because I'm getting older."

Brown spots, changes in pigment, sometimes appear. Creams and lotions are bought that promise to "erase the brown spots."

Body Shape

The body naturally changes shape in some ways. Osteoporosis creates skeletal changes such as stooped shoulders and a rounded back, and clothing doesn't fit so well. Arthritis creates gnarled fingers and/ or toes.

There may be roundness where there was once a smooth surface or less fullness where there was once roundness. These changes often occur in the areas of the chest, abdomen, or hips and thighs. In many older people, visceral fat, or "deep" fat, collects around the midsection of the body and on various internal organs, and subcutaneous fat, or fat just under the skin, diminishes in the extremities.

Exercise machines (plus a lot of work) promise to re-shape our bodies, and advertisements for undergarments promise to "hide your tummy" or "reduce your waist measurement" or "firm and shape your bosom." Some people, in an effort to reduce the effect of aging body shape changes, choose clothing styles that look as if they are designed for younger bodies. Some resort to having unwanted fat deposits removed, by having the fat sucked from the body in a procedure called liposuction, essentially a surgical procedure and not without some risks associated with surgery.

Changes in Senses

Vision

Several factors enter into the loss of vision, or impairment of vision. Although our bodies are constantly replacing old cells with new cells, and although most of the cells in our bodies are only about seven years old, the exception is the visual cortex of our brain. This is the part of the brain that interprets the signals taken in by the eyes, and it consists of the same cells we have when we are born, barring damage to the brain.

Our changes in vision are caused by the changes in our eyes themselves. The lenses harden somewhat as we age and are not as flexible and adaptable, causing us to have trouble focusing. The lens changes shape and stiffens somewhat over time, making it necessary to have glasses ground to compensate for the changes, enabling people to read smaller print.

Many people in their 40s find the print in telephone books and some newspapers beginning to seem smaller and smaller. When that happened to me, I was unprepared and thought something terrible was happening to my eyes. The ophthalmologist examined my eyes and with a somber look said, "I must tell you of a condition you have now." I squirmed in the chair, waiting for the bad news. "You have what we call 'fortyitis' and you will see better with bifocals," he said with a smile. I have learned the condition is called presbyopia, a condition occurring mostly in middle and older age, in which the lens loses elasticity, making it more difficult for the lens to dilate. My bifocal lenses made the print seem larger, making life much easier!

Cataracts occur and cloud some older people's vision, sometimes blocking light completely. If cataracts grow to a certain point, they sometimes need to be removed in order to allow a person to see more clearly.

Another vision loss that can occur among the elderly is macular degeneration. As this condition progresses, it causes things in the direct line of sight to be blurred and indistinguishable. This is a condition that cannot be cured, but some encouraging results with anti –VEGF (vascular endothelial growth factor) treatment that might slow the progression of the disease have been reported in major medical journals, including *Retina: The Journal of Retinal and Vitreous Diseases*. If macular degeneration progresses, it can severely limit people's ability to function.

Studies have shown that different problems concerning vision can affect aging people. They may have trouble processing as quickly as when they were younger, affecting the speed at which they can read and absorb information. Reading matter that moves, for instance, the type on many TV shows, or the "ticker" band at the bottom of the screen for breaking news, is more difficult for aging eyes to read.

Light often needs to be brighter than in earlier days, and night driving becomes problematic because of changes in the way aging eyes cope with glare. The rods and cones, the cells in the eyes that allow light to be interpreted, lose their ability with age. The ability to read road signs at a distance is impaired. The ability to detect and identify objects, especially in low light, seems to be diminished. Some studies indicate a decline in depth perception with age. This may affect driving ability but also possibly accounts for some falls, especially on steps, inclines or declines and any uneven surface.

Age appears to affect the way we can pick out certain important information from a "cluttered" array. For example, road signs that are mixed with billboards, neon advertising, bus stop signs, etc., become more difficult for older people to distinguish. It is as if searching for the important information takes longer and perhaps too long to make driving safe. Printed advertising with more white space is preferable if advertisers want the important points to be noticed.

Put all these vision changes together, and it becomes apparent that older people are acutely aware of the differences between what they see now and what they could see when they were younger. Eyeglasses seem to be more socially acceptable than other assistive devices, leading one advertisement for an assistive hearing device to compare wearing the device with wearing reading glasses. Pretty good marketing – appealing to pride of appearance! Even though glasses seem to be more socially acceptable, many people prefer contact lenses or laser surgery when distortions of vision can be corrected, making it unnecessary to wear glasses.

Hearing

Hearing aids broadcast to the world that one of our senses has deteriorated. Studies have shown that as we age, several changes can take place in our hearing. Some of the changes may be caused by exposure to loud noises (85 decibels or above). Exposure to loud noises, sometimes even one loud song, but certainly a lifetime of loud sound, even if it's regarded as music, can cause the hair cells in the inner ear to die, and those don't regenerate. Other changes may be caused by genetics over which people have no control.

Higher frequencies are often the first to go, hence the usefulness of lowering the pitch of your voice when speaking with someone who is hearing impaired. Volume may help in some cases, but if the voice or music is high-pitched, volume will not help. When a speaker is interrupted by another noise before continuing (for instance by a cough, sneeze, or other sound unrelated to the content) people with some hearing impairment may have trouble following the train of thought and feel they may have missed a word.

Filtering out background noise and attending to speech (selective listening), begins to become especially difficult in crowded places such as restaurants or parties. In such situations, conversation blends into the noisy environment.

Rapid speech becomes difficult for older people to comprehend and decipher. Processing time seems to slow somewhat as we age. Younger people tend to speak more rapidly, sometimes too rapidly for older adults to process and understand all the words. This, combined with the often higher pitch of young voices, can interfere with understanding the speech of a younger person, but is also noticeable when watching some modern movies. Video games and television have shortened many younger people's attention spans, and as a result their speech is often accelerated. Try watching a classic movie from the 40s or 50s and compare the rate of speech with a more recent movie aimed at a younger audience. The younger audience would probably fall asleep during the older movie because of the slow pace.

Recently I was with my husband at an eye clinic. He had cataract surgery several years ago, and it was time for a checkup. The examination was quite extensive and thorough, and while he was being examined, I had my notebook out taking notes. Besides taking notes on what was being said about his eyes, I wrote, "Young man did first stage of vision exam, spoke rapidly, did not enunciate clearly, looked away from husband as he spoke.

Much time spent asking technician to repeat. The young woman taking medical history and asking questions talked rapidly in high-pitched voice as she faced a computer screen. More time spent asking her to repeat." This is an example of how NOT to speak to older people. It causes time wasted with repetition and a high frustration level in the listener. I so wanted to do an impromptu training of the staff on how to communicate with elderly patients. As our population ages, there is a real need for trainers who can teach those in the medical service professions better, more effective ways of speaking to aging patients.

Consonants are easily confused by aging ears, because those have less energy (in technical terms) than vowels – that is, they require less vocal effort than vowels (say "gave," "seen," and "robe," and see how the sound of the vowel overshadows the sounds of the consonants). The sounds of consonants help people identify words. The consonants *p*, *t*, *k*, *b*, *d*, *m*, *n*, and *g* are often mistaken for other consonants by people whose hearing is slightly impaired. Louder speech only accentuates the vowels, and the consonants still are not heard clearly. When more emphasis, or energy, is placed on the consonant it barely raises the volume, but increases the likelihood that the consonant will be identified correctly. Enunciating slowly and pronouncing the consonants distinctly can help people with hearing loss understand what is being said. Context also helps older people identify sounds correctly, even when they are not clearly heard.

People often put off getting hearing aids for years after they are needed, because of pride in appearance, and as a result they lose out on conversations with family and friends. They resist telling other people they can't hear what is being said, and they tend to nod their heads and smile a lot. There is an old saying that other people know you need hearing aids five years before you realize it. Advertisements for hearing aids often emphasize that "they are hardly visible" or "hard to see" or "100% invisible," appealing to those who are resisting hearing aids because of appearance.

Smaller aids that fit into the ears are barely noticeable, but are not for everyone, because of their limited capacity for clarifying or enhancing sounds. The larger and more noticeable the aid, the greater effect it can have on appearance, even though it can greatly increase the enjoyment of hearing sounds well.

One of my relatives had a severe hearing loss and wore aids that were very visible. She instructed her hairdresser to make waves that covered her ears so that her hearing aids could not be seen. She felt that needing help with her hearing made her appear mentally deficient, as well as older than she felt. The ancient Greek belief that deafness indicated intellectual impairment still apparently has a residue of influence in this day and age!

Taste

With aging comes some dulling of the taste buds. More and different seasonings are required to make food taste good. While salt enhances some flavors, salt is often restricted, so some creativity must be used to bring out flavors. Our olfactory sense, or sense of smell, relates to the sense of taste, and as our sense of smell decreases in sensitivity, that also affects the way food tastes. We remember the taste of things our mother or grandmother used to cook, and the taste is not the same. Mealtime becomes a marker in the day to divide the time and to socialize, but doesn't hold the anticipation or enjoyment of eating it once did. A decrease in the enjoyment of food can result in malnutrition if food intake is not closely monitored by caregivers. A variety of colors, textures, and tastes such as sweet or sour can make eating more pleasurable for elders. The decrease in enjoyment of loved foods represents a loss.

Loss of teeth because of poor dental hygiene, gum disease, or infection can cause a change in appearance, especially if dentures are not well-crafted or if they do not fit well. Even if the change is a positive one, a person may look into the mirror and think, "That's not the real me."

Ill-fitting dentures affect the ability to eat and enjoy some foods, and they interfere with nutritional needs. Foods that are not chewed well may cause digestive problems. One of my clients said he used to enjoy apples and corn on the cob, but since he got dentures he can no longer eat those things. Having to cut the corn off the cob, while his relatives are enjoying eating it from the cob, or having to cut apples into pieces rather than biting into a whole apple, causes him to feel different and uncomfortable and interferes with his enjoyment of those foods.

Smell

The association of smell with taste has already been mentioned. The loss of the ability in some older people to detect odors makes it necessary for the caregiver to schedule baths and hygiene, as the patient may not detect body odor. He may have exercised, but not realize he and his clothing smell of perspiration. She may want to wear the same dresses, slacks, or blouses too often, not realizing they have an odor. Undergarments need to be changed each day. A resident of an assisted living community became embarrassed when her family came and went through her closet, gathering clothing that needed to be washed or cleaned. She had not realized the clothing had an offensive odor until the daughter-in-law commented that much of it "smells bad." Only then did the resident realize the extent of the loss of her sense of smell.

Safety demands that a caregiver monitor the kitchen if the patient is still cooking, because she may leave the stove or coffee pot on and not smell things burning. The decreased sense of smell may also cause older people to apply too much shaving lotion or perfume, overwhelming the people around them.

Touch

Skin thins with age, and increased pressure is required for an older person to feel and register someone's touch. Injuries to the skin may happen more easily, as it thins and tears more easily. It does not heal as quickly as when we were young.

Nerve endings decrease and that makes older people less sensitive to external pain on the body. Older persons also become less sensitive to temperature changes and care must be taken to keep the trunk from becoming too warm or the extremities from becoming too cold. Increased fat layers around the trunk keep the body from releasing heat. The fat layer underneath the skin on the extremities is reduced as we age, and we are less able to protect our extremities from cold temperatures. Very hot summers or severely cold winters may cause elders without sufficient cooling or heating in their living quarters to suffer from heat strokes or hypothermia at temperatures that would be withstood more easily by younger people. Caregivers must understand that the patient's body "thermostat" does not regulate the perception of the temperature indoors or outdoors as it did when the patient was younger. Ask any caregiver – it is not unusual to walk into a room in which the patient is comfortable, but to the caregiver the temperature in the room feels like an oven.

Bath water may feel comfortable to a caregiver, but may be too cold or too warm for an older person. Water too cool can cause chilling. Most states require nursing homes and assisted living communities to have their hot water heaters set no higher than 110-113 degrees Fahrenheit, to avoid accidentally burning elderly residents. One particularly active and alert resident of one of the assisted living communities I managed came into my office one day and said, "I want a hot shower. I'm tired of having water that is just warm. Can't you turn the temperature up?" I explained the state regulations to him and the reason for the regulations, but he was a very unhappy man. Even the temperature of his shower could not be fully regulated by him – another loss.

Changes in Health

Mobility

Mobility may become a problem requiring assistance. Pride is a big part of the mobility issue. My mother called her cane her "stick," and it hung on the handrail in her apartment most of the time rather than accompanying her when she walked. Using a cane indicated that she needed help with mobility, and that indicated she was growing older.

Many conditions call for the use of what the health industry calls an "assistive device." If health issues cause a problem with walking or moving about, there are canes, walkers, wheelchairs, or motorized "scooters" as assistive devices. They are generally looked upon with disdain by elderly people, at least at first. Many times seniors would rather chance falling than admit they need a cane or a walker.

When a cane will suffice, that is the assistive device of choice to most elderly, but even that carries a stigma. My mother, at age 86, used her "stick" with reluctance. When the time came that she needed to use a walker, she felt further stigmatized among her peers, and used it infrequently. We had borrowed my aunt's, which had to be picked up and placed in front of the person as each few steps were taken. Mother wanted a walker with small wheels on the front two legs. She became ill before one could be acquired, and was bedfast.

The hospice worker brought a walker and a wheelchair for use in Mother's apartment, if she should be able to be out of bed. The walker had small wheels on the front legs. I showed it to Mother and her eyes twinkled. "It has wheels," she said, smiling. She was never able to use it. As she lay dying, the hospice worker came to get the walker, and we refused to let him have it back until Mother's life had ended. I had a fear that she'd rally and want to see her walker "with wheels," and I didn't want to have to tell her it was gone.

There appears to be a status hierarchy among users of assistive devices – at least that is my observation after working in a number of senior communities. A pretty wooden cane is preferred by most people to a metal cane. A single stick metal cane is preferred esthetically to a metal cane with three or four prongs at the bottom.

A walker with large wheels and brakes and a fold-down seat is preferable to a walker without a seat. A walker with large wheels and brakes, even without a seat, is preferable to a metal walker with wheels on the front legs but not on the back legs. A metal walker with wheels on the front legs is preferable to a walker with no wheels that has to be picked up and placed ahead each time a step is taken.

A motorized scooter is preferable to a motorized wheelchair. A motorized wheelchair is preferable to a wheelchair that has to be pushed by using the arms to roll the wheels. And if you use a wheelchair that has to be pushed by another person, well...

What is the common denominator in this hierarchy of assistive devices? Levels of independence, indicators that at least some abilities are still intact – indication that age has not robbed people of all their mobility capabilities.

Skeletal Changes

Many people's bones become less dense and more brittle as they age, a condition called osteoporosis, and a fall or a bump can produce a fracture. As we now know, a fracture of brittle, osteoporotic bone can even be caused by a sudden stop or turn and can cause a fall. In addition, loss of strength and muscle mass with age increases the chance of falling and fracturing bones.

Once accustomed to a certain height, elders may find they are shrinking. The bones may begin to curve, especially the backbone just below the neck, producing the frequently seen "dowager's hump" in women. The vertebrae may begin to collapse, resulting in a loss of height and further stooped appearance. In extreme cases of osteoporosis, the backbone collapses to the point of obstructing breathing and digestion.

Arthritis is a condition that often causes changes in the appearance of hands, feet, and sometimes whole limbs. Gnarled fingers and hands interfere with the ability to manage certain tasks, and gnarled toes and feet interfere with the ability to find and wear comfortable shoes, as well as ambulate without pain.

Diseases, both Chronic and Acute

My aunt, a vibrant, productive woman all her life until age 70, stated once in a letter, "This is not what my golden years were supposed to be like – confined to my recliner or wheelchair in a nursing home, grieving over my body's fight with Parkinson's." Many diseases cause life changes that limit functioning and activities as well as place other limitations on a patient's lifestyle.

Some of the more common chronic conditions include arthritis, high blood pressure, heart disease, emphysema, ulcers, and diabetes. Elders may have not one, but two or more of these. While many people can live with these conditions for years, sometimes the illness can progress to an acute stage and become life-threatening.

The diagnosis of more acute diseases or conditions can come suddenly and take older people by surprise. The dreaded word by most people is "cancer" in any form.

When lab results began to show the kidney functions of my first husband, Paul, were decreasing, the doctor sent us to a nephrologist, or kidney specialist, who looked at Paul's blood report and sent us to an oncologist. The oncologist had more lab work done, studied it carefully, and performed a bone marrow biopsy. Within two days we had the diagnosis of acute myelogeneous leukemia, the most aggressive form of the four types of leukemia. Paul called me at work to tell me the oncologist had called with the diagnosis. I was with a client when the call came, but I had left word with my receptionist to interrupt me if my husband called. I heard the words, a chill settled over me, and I told Paul I would be home as soon as I could. Without a word to my client about the phone call, I finished the session in a reasonably normal fashion, had the receptionist cancel the rest of my clients for the day, and I drove home sobbing. Paul and I spent the rest of the afternoon sitting in our living room, alternately crying and staring into space, in total disbelief of how our lives had changed in just a few days.

The experience of going to the physician for a checkup and being told some serious condition exists, or that a chronic condition has morphed into an acute condition, is not as rare as we'd like to think. When that happens, the patient and the family have their world turned upside-down. The loss of stability in the now uncertain state of illness with an uncertain future creates its own form of grief. Many of the plans for the future must now be discarded and new plans made. In the next chapter on secondary losses, we will look at the fallout from experiences like these.

Muscle Tone, Strength, and Stamina

I remember my mother's lamenting that she could no longer lift the heavy sacks of fertilizer for her lawn. She had done that for years, but the day came when she had to have help to lift a sack. A neighbor provided the help, but it was a symbolic loss to my mother, a loss of the ability to be as physically able as before.

As we age, muscle mass decreases, and something as simple as opening a jar becomes difficult, signaling the decline of strength and muscle tone. Shopping becomes a chore as stamina decreases. Recreational activities once enjoyed become too tiring. Exercise can help, but many have other health issues that prevent or greatly curtail the amount of exercise that can be performed.

Memory

As we age, there may be a slight delay in the ability to process or retrieve information, and the delay can be frustrating. Though not inevitable, this can be a normal progression of aging and does not significantly interfere with a person's functioning. When a decline in memory is noticed by family and friends and the decline is diagnosed as dementia, this becomes an adjustment that is very difficult, both for the patient and for the people who interact with him.

This loss will be discussed more fully in Chapter 8, on dementia, but for now, we'll just say that losing one's memory to Alzheimer's disease or another type of dementia means losing everything a person holds dear. She can stay alive physically for years, but eventually loses the ability to relate to people or objects in a meaningful way.

Emotional Changes

Loss of Family Members

As we age, we inevitably have loved ones who die. The natural progression is to lose parents, then siblings and/or spouse. Some people may have experienced the loss of a child. However, as people live longer, the likelihood increases that they may experience the death of an adult child or the death of a grandchild.

Losing parents, even though in the natural order of things, represents a significant loss for people as they age. Transitions include thinking of oneself as an orphan; being one notch closer to death in the natural order; and eventually becoming the age parents were when they died, thus feeling more and more vulnerable, and feeling twinges of guilt that we lived longer than they did. I remember reaching the age of 58, the age at which my father died, and each year thereafter thinking, "I'm older than my dad ever was." It was sobering.

Siblings are the people with whom we share most of the years of our lives, and the death of a sibling represents the loss not only of the person, but also a great deal of our family history. One of my clients lamented, "I am the last of six brothers and sisters, and it is a very lonely feeling. We used to reminisce about our childhood when we got together, and now I have no one to talk to about that. They remembered things I had forgotten, and vice-versa."

Losing a spouse after many years of marriage can be devastating. I have counseled many widows and widowers, but nine years ago I experienced this loss firsthand when my husband, Paul, died of leukemia. We had known each other since we were children, and our marriage was a very happy one. His struggle with leukemia for three and a half years, knowing the battle would likely be won by the disease, was one of the most difficult things we had ever been through. He was courageous and rarely complained during that time. I could hardly stand the thought of losing him, but I knew it was inevitable. He made it to our 50th wedding anniversary and was able to enjoy the family dinner and celebration planned by our children, but he died seven months later. He died peacefully, after having had private visits with each of our children. He and I had talked a lot and said all we wanted and needed to say to each other. He even graciously encouraged me to marry again so I wouldn't be alone.

It is one thing to know death is around the corner, it is quite another thing to realize the last breath has been taken. When Paul stopped breathing, my life changed forever. I lost my best friend, my lover, my companion, and my children's father in one instant. At that instant the world seemed to stop revolving. Even now as I write about that event, I had to stop for a moment, as that memory is still so vivid, and it seems the world stopped revolving once again for a few seconds. The entire story of Paul's illness and death is for another book, but I know how utterly alone a spouse can feel at the death of the other. So many older people have lost spouses, some of them more than one.

The death of a child of any age can be a surreal experience. None of us expects to outlive our children. Mine and Paul's second child, four-year-old Cathy, died of a sudden, short illness when Paul and I were both in our twenties. Somehow we survived that experience, and we matured much faster because of it. It forever erased the fantasy with which most parents enter parenthood, that we can protect our children from harm, and that if we don't, we have failed as parents. Once one of your children dies, you realize you are not immune to any of life's tragedies. You never get over it; you simply learn to cope with it.

Losing an adult child becomes more common as people age. In an assisted living community I managed, I got a call from a resident's son that his brother had died, and he asked me to go to his mother's apartment and give her the sad news. She was a small woman of 86. She had lost so much already, and now I had to say, "Mabel, Howard just called and asked me to come visit with you. You remember your son Walter has been very sick after a heart attack. This morning Walter's heart completely failed, and he has died." Mabel's face contorted with grief. Walter was 62 years old, her first child. She said, "I remember when he was born. He was so chubby, and we were so proud of him. We named him for my uncle." I could almost see her mind rewinding the memories of long ago. Gently I said, "Howard will be here later today to take you to the funeral home to help him with the arrangements. He wanted me to come and tell you and be with you for a while. Can I make us some tea?" Losing an adult child with a lifetime of memories takes a great toll on a parent.

Grandchildren's deaths take a toll, but research has shown that grandparents grieve more for the pain the parents are experiencing than for the loss of the grandchild, although of course there is also a great deal of grief over the grandchild's death. Grandparents feel helpless to take away the pain of their child who has lost a child. We always want to protect our children from pain, and in the case of their losing a child, we are helpless to protect them.

Losing a spouse through divorce can be devastating, because it signifies the death of a relationship that was once cherished. Whether the divorce was chosen, or a mutual decision, or imposed upon one, the loss of the relationship is a cause for grief.

Loss of Pets

Pets may be lost through death, but sometimes are lost by their owner's having to relocate to a place where pets are not welcome. Either way, the loss of a companion of a number of years can have a severe impact and cause a major grief response. In later years a pet may provide companionship, satisfy the need to be needed by another living thing, provide an opportunity for nurturing, and give unconditional love. Many people think of their pets as their children or best friends or mascots, talking to them, holding and cuddling them, feeding them, taking them to the vet. These responsibilities give meaning to the later years, and the loss of those responsibilities causes grief. Studies have shown that pets actually have beneficial effects on people's physical and mental health. Stroking a pet can lower blood pressure and cholesterol levels. Some research has shown that people who have cats seem to have fewer psychiatric disturbances. "Animals enrich our lives. Anyone who has ever cared for an animal knows that the more we give to them, the more they give us in return," according to author A.M. Schoen. Losing a loved pet triggers the grief response.

Death of Peers

Sometimes the death of one's peers can impact a person as much or more than the loss of a relative. We choose our friends, whereas our relatives are thrust upon us by nature. Our friends are more likely to have shared many of the details of our lives that we didn't feel comfortable sharing with our family. Our peers are sometimes more like us in interests than are family members. Too, our peers are closer to our own age, thereby causing us to ponder our own mortality.

One of my friends from graduate school died suddenly from a heart attack. We had become very close, were close in age, went to meetings together, made joint presentations at conferences, and went on vacations together with our husbands. Her funeral was in another city in another state, and my husband and I traveled there. We were not asked to sit with the family, but I felt almost like family. We sat with the "other friends," but I felt none of them had known her as well as I had. After the funeral, I stood by my husband on the porch of the church and sobbed uncontrollably – some of it for the loss of my friend, some of it because I felt left out, and some of it for my own sense of mortality. There will be more about these kinds of peer losses in the chapter on disenfranchised grief.

Retirement

Retiring from a career can affect income and social status, and sometimes results in social isolation. Unless adequate steps have been taken to prepare financially for retirement, there may be a severe change in lifestyle. If work has been a significant part of a person's identity, which it often is, his perception of his status may be lower, even if his retirement is not viewed by others as a decrease in status.

One of my clients who was processing the transition into retirement said, "What do I say when I'm asked, 'What do you do?' Do I list the retirement activities that fill the void left by quitting work? Or do I say, 'I used to…'" It was as if he had lost a piece of himself when he left his life-long profession.

Working also often produces a camaraderie that is satisfying. When no longer involved with co-workers, sometimes a deep loss is experienced, even when people had looked forward to retiring and thought no longer having to work would be wonderful. This may surprise persons who had looked forward to retirement and had not realized the loss of the social aspect.

As we move on to Chapter 3 and the subject of secondary losses, keep in mind that the list of primary losses I have outlined is not all-inclusive by any means. It is merely an attempt to enlarge the concept of grief and loss and to show how many losses can combine to create life-long grief for people as they age.

CHAPTER 3

Understanding the Secondary Losses

SECONDARY LOSSES ARE CHANGES BROUGHT about as a result of primary losses. This is where the circular part of the experiences of loss begins. I warned you earlier that it can seem more circular than linear, but since we are stuck with going through it in linear fashion, I must simply remind you of the circular aspect. Secondary losses apply to so many primary losses that you will notice some repetition, but I'm afraid if I leave out things that apply to a specific secondary loss, it will not provide an accurate account of the effects of multiple losses. Read on, and you'll soon see what I mean.

LOSS OF PHYSICAL ABILITIES
AFFECTED BY: CHANGES IN HEALTH; DISEASE OR ACCIDENT; LOSS OF MEMORY.

People who were athletes suffer loss when they realize they are not able to run, ski, catch a ball, or swim as well as they once did. Imagine a man who loved to fish, but whose health prevents his going fishing; a long-distance runner who now has severe arthritis in his knees and can no longer walk without pain, let alone run; someone who used to knit beautiful sweaters but now cannot manage the needles because of paralysis following a stroke; a patient who used to sing in a choir but who developed cancer of the larynx or who had a stroke and can no longer speak, much less sing; someone who is aware of her increasing loss of memory and who used to be a whiz at accounting. Think about what you enjoy and how you would feel if you were no longer able to enjoy that activity.

When the home and lawn maintenance or household duties become more than homeowners can manage, they have to ask for help. I remember when my grandfather had to admit he could no longer keep up with his lawn and had to ask my cousins to mow and trim for him. He sat on the porch in a lawn chair and "supervised," but even as a child I recognized the sadness in his face.

When cognitive function begins to fade, as in many forms of dementia, a person recognizes she is no longer able to keep up with her peers in many ways. Abilities formerly enjoyed are often forgotten. Feeling inadequate without knowing exactly why, she may withdraw rather than try to keep up. More will be said about this stage in the chapter on dementia.

Loss of Roles
Affected by: Loss of spouse or partner; loss of child; retirement; loss of physical abilities; loss of memory.

The loss of roles, or "parts we play in life," can be a cause of grief. For instance, if a spouse or partner dies or if a divorce occurs, we are no longer a wife or husband or part of a couple. The ring may still be worn after a spouse's death, but realistically the marriage role is no longer a part of who you are. Many people struggle with this role loss when their spouse or partner dies or when they divorce. One client wore her wedding band five years after her husband's death. One day she said, "I guess it's time to take it off, but it marks the end of my being a wife. Now I'm only half of who I was." The loss of that role was very important to her and affected her grieving.

When an only child dies, parents feel they suffer the loss of their parenthood. Many times clients ask, "Am I still a parent? What do I say when people ask if I have children?" They are affected by no longer having the role of "parent," especially when they are around other parents.

Even people who have other children wonder how they should speak about a child who is deceased. Do they mention only the living children, or do they say, "I have [number of] living children," implying they have had more. Each child is important, and they hate ignoring the fact that another child was a part of their family at one time. A part of their role as parent was involved with that child while he or she was alive.

Retirement often means the loss of a role. If someone worked 40 years as a machinist, but now has retired from that career, is he still a machinist? Or is he a "former machinist"? If a person worked 40 years as a secretary, but now has retired from that career, is she still a secretary? Or is she a "former secretary"? For people whose identity was wrapped up in their vocation, this represents a severe loss. Retirement often changes people's perception of themselves.

G. Stanley Hall, a psychologist and the founding president of Clark University in Massachusetts, wrote an article (anonymously) at age 77 for Atlantic Monthly in 1921, entitled "Old Age," in which he lamented, "After well-nigh, half a century of almost unbroken devotion to an exacting vocation, I lately retired." He went on to say, "It seemed at first like anticipatory death and the press notices of my withdrawal read to me not unlike obituaries." Later, "I…had had moments of idealizing the leisure retirement would bring; but now that it has come, I am overwhelmed and almost disoriented by its completeness, and am at a loss how to use it… Now I am divorced from my world, and there is nothing more to be said of me save the exact date of my death, and men who retire often die soon afterward..." Clearly, retirement affected this man's perception of himself, and clearly he was grieving the loss of his role.

Loss of Financial Status
Affected by: Loss of spouse or partner; changes in health; retirement.

You might be surprised to learn that many survivors do not know anything about their financial situation as a couple. I have had widows in my office who have had to be taught to write a check. Balancing a checkbook is foreign to them. They have no idea what kinds of investments their husband had arranged.

This feeling of inadequacy affects their self-esteem, but often their financial status as well, especially if their resources have not been managed well. Some survivors find they are deeply in debt, when they had no idea. When their spouse or partner dies, they may find they have to manage on less income, particularly if both were receiving Social Security benefits, because the amount will be reduced by a formula Social Security uses. If the spouse or partner was still working, that source of income is gone, and the survivor may have to find a job to make ends meet.

Some have had spouses or partners who required a great deal of medical care, racking up a pile of bills that have to be paid. Some people spend a great deal of money to try to make life as pleasant for the sick spouse or partner as possible and in doing so, deplete their resources. When the spouse or partner dies, the survivor is left with the grief, but also a huge debt load.

If a person is working and has to take early retirement, either because of company policies or because of health issues, the loss of income will affect his financial status, and may affect his self-esteem.

Loss of Self-esteem
Affected by: Changes in appearance; loss of roles; loss of memory; retirement; loss of financial status.

Our feelings about ourselves can be affected by natural changes in appearance, discussed in an earlier chapter. Feeling less attractive affects our self-esteem. For those to whom appearance has been a very important part of their personality, it takes inordinate effort for them to compensate.

When my mother lived in a retirement apartment community, I visited often, checking to be sure she had taken her medication on schedule and filling her pill box with her daily doses for the next week. When my husband and I scheduled a two-week vacation, I enlisted the help of the staff to check on her and make sure she took her medications each morning. In order to accommodate each resident, the staff began rounds about 6:00 a.m., often waking a resident to administer her pills for the day. Most of the residents then would sleep for a while longer.

When we returned from our trip, I asked Mother how things had gone while we were away. "Well, I'm relieved you're back, because now I can take my pills when I want to. I had to set my alarm for 5:30 every morning so I could get up, dress, comb my hair, put in my hearing aids, and put on my makeup before time for them to come around with my pills. I didn't want them to come in here while I was still in bed and see what I look like when I have just waked up!" Obviously, appearance was very important to her self-esteem. Remember, she is the woman who, in earlier years, plucked her first grey hairs with the tweezers until she realized she'd never keep up with them.

Loss of self-esteem is experienced in various degrees as graying or thinning hair, baldness, declining senses such as hearing and vision, wrinkles, or body shape affect the way people view themselves. Add moving more slowly; having to use a cane, walker, wheelchair, or motorized scooter; shrinking height; gnarled hands and/or feet; and dentures, and you begin to see the many ways appearance can affect people's self-esteem as they age.

Add to the equation lowered financial status, loss of memory, and loss of career role in retirement. Some people have a difficult time adjusting to these losses and suffer blows to their self-esteem.

Loss of Ability to Drive
Affected by: Changes in health, changes in senses, loss of memory.

The loss of the ability to drive has been shown by some studies to be more devastating to a person than the death of a spouse. That day when the keys are taken away marks the day he loses his independence. This loss usually comes about through changes in health, changes in senses such as vision or hearing, or loss of memory. The loss of the ability to drive deprives a person of the freedom to go where he wants to go, and requires him to be dependent on others for transportation. Knowing his vehicle has been sold is often a traumatic event for him, as it is a final marker that means he is now dependent. It is no surprise that in advertisements for senior communities, often there is mention of parking spaces, carports, or garages. Some who move there will still be able to drive, but many of those who can no longer drive want to imagine themselves driving again someday.

One daughter, whose father was developing dementia and could also no longer see well, said, "Dad, why don't we just sell the car?" He became very indignant and said, "No, I need that car. I like looking out there and knowing I have it." After the daughter left, with his car keys in her hand, tears streamed down her face, as she knew he could no longer safely drive, but he still insisted on keeping the car. Independence is a very difficult thing with which to part.

Loss of Independence
Affected by: Changes in health; loss of memory in either self, spouse, or partner; loss of a spouse or partner; loss of ability to drive.

A person's independence is often suddenly affected by changes in health or loss of a spouse or partner. His health can deteriorate quickly, causing him to be dependent on others for many things. When my first husband, a formerly robust man who flew across the country each week during his career, developed leukemia and began chemotherapy, the adjustment he faced was tremendous. Instead of leading his usually active life, he now was dependent on physicians, nurses, and me for his care. He reacted with grace, but it was a difficult transition for him.

Memory loss in either a person or his spouse or partner can change a person's degree of independence. If a spouse or partner begins to develop dementia and needs a great deal of care, no longer can the other decide on the spur of the moment to do something. He will be responsible for his spouse's or partner's comfort and welfare when planning an activity or trip, even to the grocery store. In the case of his own memory loss, he will be dependent on someone else.

Loss of ability to drive has been discussed, but loss of the person who provided transportation is also possible. My mother-in-law never did learn to drive. She said it made her nervous. She depended on my father-in-law to do the driving. When he died suddenly of a heart attack, his death took away not only her husband, but also her handy availability of transportation. In addition, she had been recovering from a stroke, and he had been her caregiver. In the absence of someone close by to care for her, she agreed to move into a nursing home. Multiple situations combined suddenly to affect her independence within a short time.

Loss of Environment

Affected by: Death of spouse or partner; changes in health of spouse or partner; loss of financial status; memory loss in self, spouse, or partner.

A loss many people don't recognize is the loss of familiar environment. We become comfortable in our environment – our apartment or home, our neighborhood, our town or city, and our state, but sometimes this environment changes.

The death or illness of a spouse or partner can often cause a change in environment. If a spouse or partner needs care and the couple decides to move together to an assisted living community or to a nursing home, or if a spouse or partner dies and the surviving spouse cannot live alone and needs care, a change of environment occurs, often very quickly. Remember my mother-in-law's changes in just a matter of days. It can be to a senior community, to live with family members, or to live nearer to family. Leaving a familiar home of many years, memories associated with that home, neighborhood and neighbors, and familiar shopping areas are difficult enough even when changing residences within the same town or city. Add to that the fact that often relocation takes people out of the town or city with which they are familiar.

When a friend of mine was widowed some years ago, she decided to move to a different state to be near her children. She did not anticipate all the adjustments she would have to make besides those listed above. She found different weather patterns that hindered her outdoor activities, she found the people talked differently, she found she was allergic to some of the vegetation in the area, and as she wrote me, "Even the state flag is different!" That was her attempt at humor in summing up the differences and her displeasure with them.

If people must move into a retirement community, they are faced with meeting all new fellow residents plus staff members, and their surroundings are quite different. They find they may not be able to control the temperature in their room or apartment. They have to adjust to a structured mealtime and to many other rules of the management. They will find the water for showers is not as hot as they would like. They miss their friends, the control, and the privacy they had in their own home. One patient told me, "I have to live with all these *old* people! Some of them smell bad."

If people move in with children or other family members, they may feel "in the way" or like a burden. They find the rules of the house are different from the rules of their own house. They may have to adjust to eating different foods if their favorites do not happen to be favorites of the family. They may not have control over what is watched on the television, so may miss some of their favorite programs. They may have to adjust to being around young children or teenagers again and lots of noise. They may have no real "alone time" or privacy; or, perhaps if the family is gone all day, they may have too much alone time.

If health issues are not the reason for needing to relocate, sometimes the reason is financial. With one income instead of two, the house payment or rent may be too much for the surviving person to afford, and moving to a less expensive house or apartment in a different part of town may be necessary. Some may find this unsatisfactory.

Whatever the reason for relocating, many are the losses associated with such a move. Environment is a large part of our comfort, and when the environment changes dramatically, the losses are great. These are losses that are not easily recognized or validated by others.

Loss of Social Status

Affected by: Loss of spouse or partner; loss of environment; change in abilities; loss of financial status; loss of memory in self, spouse, or partner.

Many newly single persons find they are excluded from social gatherings of couples, and it often comes as a complete surprise. Even close friends often "forget" to include the now-single person in their social gatherings. Sometimes it is because of insecurities that make couples fearful of having someone "who is now available" in their midst. Sometimes it is because it brings their own mortality too close for comfort. Whatever the reason, many who lose their spouse or partner find themselves suddenly "left out."

Another loss of social status often occurs when persons move into a retirement community, an assisted living community, or a nursing home. Many times they are not included in social invitations as they once were. Possibly others see that as forecasting their own future, and it is uncomfortable to them. Whatever the reason, when I worked in assisted living communities I heard various versions of the lament, "I'm not asked out as much as when I lived at home. I think my friends have forgotten about me."

Changes in ability can affect social status, as it is more time-consuming to accommodate someone who walks more slowly, or takes more time eating, or doesn't hear well, or who uses a walker or wheelchair. Friends who cannot or will not make these accommodations will soon disappear, leaving the older person feeling alone and forgotten.

A lowering of financial status often affects people's social status, as friends realize the person or couple can no longer afford the entertainments they formerly engaged in together. Sometimes friends don't know how to relate to that situation. When that happens, the invitations and visits get fewer and fewer, and the differences in financial status become an isolating issue.

When memory loss occurs, friends can be uncomfortable with that and don't know how to act or what to say, either to the one with memory loss or to the spouse or partner. What they don't realize is that they can just be themselves, engaging in normal conversation. The couple may not be invited to functions because of the discomfort of those attending. The spouse or partner without memory loss feels isolated and alone most of the time and misses the social interaction.

Each of these situations causes loneliness, feelings of abandonment, disappointment, and depression. Much depression could be alleviated with more socialization.

Loss of Sexual Opportunity/Ability
Opportunity affected by: Loss of spouse or partner; loss of spouse's or partner's memory; loss of environment.
Ability affected by: Changes in health; memory loss.

When a spouse or partner dies, it usually deprives the surviving one of sexual opportunity for a time. The loss of a spouse's or partner's memory can also affect the opportunity.

One couple who lived in an assisted living community had an apartment together for several months, but when the wife became too demented to recognize her husband or interact with other residents and began walking out the door of the building when no one was looking, the time came for her to be admitted to the dementia care unit for her safety. Her husband, a man with domineering and controlling behavior, would go and get her from the dementia care unit, take her to his apartment, and attempt to have sex with her. She would scream and cry, and had no idea what was going on. Other residents could hear her screaming, "Who are you? Get out of here!" Adult Protective Services were called in to protect her, and afterward the husband was allowed to visit her in the dementia unit only under supervision.

A similar case developed in a nursing home, where a husband shared a room with his wife, who had dementia. The husband attempted to sleep with his wife against her will, and she came running out of the room, yelling, "Who is that man in my bed?"

The issue of privacy in a retirement community inhibits couples who live in separate rooms or apartments from engaging in sexual activity, for several reasons. One reason is that other residents can be very judgmental of such couplings when the two people are not "officially" a couple. The subculture of a community is like a very small town, and what goes on often becomes "everyone's business." In an assisted living community I managed, one male resident lived next door to a female resident, and they sat together at meals in the main dining room. Once day while both residents were in the dining room, one of the housekeepers came into my office and asked me to follow her. I did. The housekeepers were not supposed to move furniture to clean, but in the woman's apartment something dropped behind a large overstuffed chair, so the housekeeper moved the chair enough to retrieve the item. When she did, she saw that the chair had been covering a large opening in the wall. It was a passageway between the two apartments. I had the unpleasant task of calling both residents into my office and notifying them that the passageway had been discovered and must be repaired at their expense.

Another reason sexual activity may be inhibited in any type of retirement community is that because of the necessity for safety, several employees may have keys to the apartments or rooms and may enter at any time. They are supposed to knock before entering, but if the residents have hearing problems, they may not hear the knock. Attendants sometimes walk in for housekeeping or maintenance or food service, and both the attendant and the couple are very surprised, and all are embarrassed.

The proportion of women to men in the later years causes most women to be left with no opportunity for sexual expression. Many family members are disapproving at the thought of their older relative engaging in sexual activity, even though the desire for closeness and physical touching usually lasts throughout life. I have been referring to people living in senior communities, but a patient being cared for at home often has no opportunity at all for sexual expression.

The ability to engage in and enjoy sex can be affected by changes in health. Many men are unable to have an erection in older age, even with the development of the medications that are supposed to be remedies for this condition. This represents a loss of "manhood" to many men, and the effect on their self-esteem is devastating. Other health issues and medications to treat diseases or conditions can cause people to lose sexual desire, but they remember what it was like, and suffer the loss nevertheless.

Memory loss in advanced stages often causes both men and women to forget how to have sex. In addition, women's hormonal changes during or after menopause often cause vaginal dryness and pain associated with intercourse and cause them to lose interest in intimacy. All these situations represent the loss of something that was once enjoyable and a function of youth.

Loss of Relationships

Affected by: Loss of spouse or partner; loss of spouse's or partner's memory; loss of environment; loss of family members; loss of peers.

Obviously, a relationship is lost when someone important to a person dies. However, a relationship is also lost for the most part when a spouse or partner makes the journey into dementia and no longer recognizes family members.

When a move is necessary because of one of the primary losses, the relationships with friends and neighbors, and even family, are affected. It is not so easy to visit, and often the strength of the relationships is gradually lost, or at least diminished. (I hope you are beginning to be more aware of the circular nature of all these losses.)

Sad to say, family conflict sometimes deprives people of relationships. My grandmother had two daughters besides my mother. The other two daughters had some kind of long-standing rift and wouldn't be in the same place at the same time. I'm not sure either of them even remembered the original situation that caused the estrangement, but they had not spoken for decades. This deprived my grandmother of family get-togethers with all members present, and deprived her of being able to speak about one daughter when the other was around. She was in constant turmoil, because she stayed part of the year with each daughter. When she died, one daughter stayed away from the funeral because she knew the other would be there. They never reconciled.

When important relationships are affected, depression may be the result. Strong social and relationship connections have been shown to lower depression.

Loss of Possessions

Affected by: Loss of spouse or partner; loss of spouse's or partner's memory; loss of environment.

For this topic, think about your own possessions and list your top 10 or 15. Stop and do it now, and keep it in front of you until you finish this section about possessions.

When someone is faced with the necessity of moving from a house into smaller quarters, because of the death or health of a spouse or partner, because of her own health, because of financial constraints, or because of the control of family members, the harsh reality of having to pare down belongings hits. Imagine, if you still live in your home, having to choose only a few pieces of furniture that will fit into the new space, or in the case of a nursing home, only a few possessions – whatever will fit into a small closet and night stand or perhaps, if you're lucky and have a larger room, a chest of drawers or dresser. As you look around and see the treasures you've acquired through the years, you quickly realize that making the decision about what to dispose of and what to take with you to your new home could be overwhelming. Pictures of family – albums or framed pictures – often fill shelves in the former home. What if you are faced with room for only a few in the new living quarters? What about the quilts that mother or grandmother made? What about the family treasures that have been passed down through the generations? Yes, they can be handed down to children or nieces or nephews, but the loss to the elderly person is the same – she is no longer the "owner." Also, often family members don't want the items and may not treasure them as much as the owner feels they should. Holiday decorations must be pared down, libraries of books disposed of with only a few choice ones retained, and familiar and much-used kitchen tools and dishes have to be discarded. Antique furniture may be too large and may not fit into the new environment. After moving into a retirement apartment, one woman surveyed her small storage closet and said, "Is that all I have left? I am a nothing." Her possessions had been an important part of her identity and represented a tremendous loss to her.

Sometimes well-meaning people try to help the griever cope with the loss of possessions by saying things like, "They were only *things*," or "You can collect some other things that don't take up so much room," or "The people you gave them to will make good use of them." These efforts do not validate the griever's feelings and are rarely comforting, because although the possessions may have been only *things*, they were *her* things, and were precious to her. Even though they took up a lot of room, they were important to her. Even though other people may be able to make good use of them, she remembers the time when *she* could make good use of them, too.

Now go back to the list of your own possessions you made when you began reading about this topic. If you are like most people, you had a difficult time prioritizing what you value most. The list of the top 10 or 15 possessions may have been changed a few times as you wrote and as other valued items came to mind. This was one of the exercises included in the training of new employees in the assisted living communities I managed. The emphasis for new staff was to be patient with residents who were actually faced with these choices, and to respect the few possessions they had decided to bring with them to the community.

People going through the process of choosing among their treasures need to be allowed to express their sadness at the loss of their possessions and have their grief validated without having their feelings dismissed. They are suffering a grief response and deserve to be listened to and supported with sympathy and understanding by the staff and family members.

Loss of Religious Connections
Affected by: Changes in health; loss of ability to drive; loss of spouse, partner, or another person who provided transportation.

People who derive much of their satisfaction from being a part of a religious group suffer a great loss when their health does not permit their attending, or when they do not have a way to get there. Their spouse or partner may have been their source of transportation, they may no longer be able to drive themselves there, and they hate having to ask someone to take them. When they move to a different locale, even if there are services available to them either in the retirement community or near their new home, they may miss the church, synagogue, or other place of worship to which they were accustomed. Religious associations are sources of strength for many people. When they are deprived of their familiar place of worship and socializing with their church friends, it is a deep loss.

Loss of Control
Affected by: Changes in health; loss of environment; loss of spouse or partner.

When elderly become dependent upon either family or retirement communities for the timing and content of meals and the timing and places of errands, for example, they suffer a lack of control that may be very new to them. When entirely independent, people can eat when they please and what they please and go where they want to go, when they want to go. Adjustment to a regimen ordered by other people is often difficult and leaves the elderly feeling helpless and frustrated.

People who experience lack of control sometimes have symptoms that don't necessarily seem related to this lack. People who fail to eat their food at meals, or those who eat too much or try to sneak food into their room are exerting some of the only control they feel they have, that of controlling their intake and/or possession of food.

Hoarding is another form of control. In an assisted living community I managed, one resident refused to let the housekeeper into her apartment to clean for a couple of weeks. When I went to talk to the woman about the need for letting the housekeeper clean her apartment, I found there was no room to sit, as every surface was covered with newspapers, magazines, and junk mail. When I tried to clear a place to sit, she informed me that what I was moving was "very important," and she did not want to misplace it. She was making a symbolic statement that "I can keep whatever I want to keep, wherever I want to keep it, and no one can tell me I can't."

For safety's and cleanliness' sake, I had to tell her she had to clean up the papers, and we would help her. In order to help her feel more in control of other things, the housekeepers and activities director were instructed to allow her to have more choices. She was allowed to set the weekly day for cleaning her apartment, with the provision that she would let the housekeeper do her job and she would dispose of any excess papers. She was allowed to "sponsor" (suggest) some activities of her choice and invite other residents to join her, and the activities director would assist her in planning these events. She still kept more papers than the average person, but as her sense of control was increased in other areas, she was able to keep her paper collection to a minimum and keep it in one place, on her desk.

I must add a disclaimer here – eating problems and hoarding are examples of complex behavioral issues and are not often solved by simple measures. My point is that in the case of the elderly, as their sense of control diminishes, often they attempt to exert whatever control they can muster, and these are things they can easily choose to try to control.

I have already discussed the reasons people need to be cared for by others – remember the circularity of this whole section. They may not have the freedom to choose where they live, but there are other choices they can be allowed to make.

Control is somewhat akin to independence or freedom, but different in some ways. Even those who are somewhat dependent need freedom to make their own decisions, about what clothing and colors to wear, what shoes are comfortable, and what they like to eat, what they like to read, which TV programs they want to watch, and what music they listen to. They can have freedom to select what they want hung on their walls, which visitors they entertain, and the colors and design of their bedding. These may seem like small things, but to people who are dependent on others for much of their care, these things can be areas of control they can maintain.

They may get verbally abusive in an attempt to exert control over others. If this is seen as a control issue because they have lost control in so many other areas of their lives, some of the personal sting may be overlooked by the people around them. Look for ways they can have some control in some areas.

These behaviors are sometimes seen in people who are developing dementia. They are losing control of their thinking processes. Similar behaviors are also sometimes seen in patients who are terminally ill. They have lost control of staying alive, and that is a fearful loss.

Loss of Individuality
Affected by: Changes in health, loss of social status, loss of environment.

Elderly are considered one big group by some, losing sight of the fact that people are no more alike as they age than they were when younger. Many elderly are still vibrant and active, but to some people the word "elderly" carries with it a vision of frail people in poor health. Browse the birthday greeting card area when you have a few minutes. The themes of humor for cards aimed at older people are often frailties – becoming hard of hearing, losing their eyesight, losing their memory, developing creaky bones and joints, increasing inability to reach the bathroom in time, etc. Ageism is alive and well in the greeting card industry.

Living in a senior community necessarily carries more rules than independent living, and structures residents' lives, causing them to feel as if they are considered a homogenous group. While one might like to lounge around and drink coffee and read the newspaper in the mornings, breakfast is served at a certain time. While one might like to watch a certain TV program in the evening, dinner is served at a certain time. While one might like to have his room painted a certain color, allowances for that kind of individuality are rarely made. Also, younger people talk in generalities about the "elderly." They may be lumped together in the minds of others as a group, although studies show older people retain their innate individuality as they age. Few generalities can accurately be made about "older people."

Loss of Youth
Affected by: Loss of appearance, changes in health, loss of abilities.

The media remind elderly daily of the youthful world and how we can "regain our youth," creating a mindset that "young is better." Advertisements display youthful bodies, skin, hair, abilities. Articles often contain ageist statements, subtle, but having an effect. One I saw recently was an advertisement for a computer for older people that is "simple to operate." The pitch was "Not your grandchild's computer," implying that older people as a group are not able to work on a regular computer. I know people in their 80s who are adept at operating and understanding a computer – and I'm sure there are some older than that.

Loss of Sources of Affection
Affected by: Loss of spouse or partner, loss of environment, loss of pet.

We're talking affection here, not particularly physical. If you had loving parents, their loss deprived you of affection, and all you have are memories. The loss of a spouse or partner, siblings, and various family members add to the loss of sources of affection. If children or relatives live at a distance, too far to visit often, face-to-face affection is minimal. As we age, some of our loved friends move away or die.

The loss of a pet, either because the pet dies or because living conditions or health prevent the older person from having a pet with them, represents the loss of a friend, often considered a "best friend." One of the retirement apartment complexes I managed allowed residents to have pets if the resident was able to care for the pet. When one resident's dog died, the man was never again his happy, social former self, and became a recluse, preferring to stay in his apartment most of the time.

These losses leave a patient with few sources of affection. She may become attached to her caregivers, but if the ties that have bound her to loving family and friends and pets are severed by distance or death, she suffers a loss.

Loss of Dignity
Affected by: Changes in health, loss of control, loss of environment.

When a patient needs care, privacy is compromised, simply because the act of caring for someone's personal needs requires a degree of intimacy that is uncomfortable to the patient. Performing these services can be done in a professional manner without compromising the patient's dignity any more than is necessary.

When I was leaving from visiting a client in a nursing home, I was horrified to witness a caregiver taking a woman from the shower room to her room in a wheelchair, with a towel wrapped loosely around her, leaving little to the imagination. I spoke to the head nurse about it on my way out, and her response was, "The caregivers are always pressured to get many showers done during the morning, and they don't always take time to be careful about privacy. I'll speak to them."

Caregivers can be thoughtless and speak to residents in ways that are demeaning and disrespectful. I wish all caregivers could be trained not to do this, but often they talk to older people as if they were children, calling them "Hon" or "Sweetie," with a little pat on the shoulder. These are adults, and they should not lose their dignity just because they grow older. This occurs in public places, as well as in the caregiving situation.

Once I had lunch with an older friend at a restaurant, and when the friend paid her bill, the cashier said, "Thank you, sweetie." My friend said nicely, "My name is Susan [not her real name], and if you are going to address me with a word, unless you know me well, I prefer to be called by my name." The cashier apologized.

AWARENESS OF THE LOSS OF TIME AFFECTED BY: LOSS OF SPOUSE OR PARTNER OR SOMEONE ELSE IMPORTANT.

The death of someone close to a person can trigger thoughts of his own mortality. He may anticipate dying himself, and with that, feel a pressure to get things done before he dies. When we realize the biological clock is ticking toward the end of our lives, we realize we have a finite number of years to live. Aging and perceiving life as "only 20 years left" or "only 10 years left," and realizing there is a finite amount of time left to accomplish whatever there is to be accomplished can be either an inspiring or a depressing realization. We feel the projects or plans we have begun must be finished, but maybe there are many more projects or plans than can ever be completed in the number of years left. Perhaps you've wanted to write your life story or write another kind of book, or organize the family pictures, or make that quilt, or travel to places you've always wanted to visit, but you realize that at least some of your aspirations will never be accomplished. The grief of unattainable goals descends.

LOSS OF HOPES AND DREAMS
AFFECTED BY: ALL CUMULATIVE LOSSES DISCUSSED.

Gather all the losses that have been mentioned, put them into an imaginary bag, and no matter what kind of pretty ribbon you might tie on the bag, the contents of that bag represents the loss of some of the hopes and dreams of older people, and the cumulative effect cannot be underestimated. Not all older people have all these losses, but many of them have multiple losses that affect their lives.

To close this chapter, I will share a recent email from my 89-year-old brother-in-law in Denver, CO, who knows I am writing this book: "Getting old is really a disease; so many bodily ailments, and mental, too. A buddy I went to grade school with, a retired pediatrician, phoned me yesterday to commiserate about the limitations of aging. He suffered a stroke a few years back and has trouble speaking. He also suffers from peripheral neuropathy, which has made climbing stairs impossible. I, of course, have a severe hearing impairment, which cuts down on the things I can do and enhances my sense of isolation. But I'm still vertical, thank God, and walk every day."

Coping with loss and the accompanying grief takes energy, often energy that older people no longer possess. Some people have a greater degree of resiliency than others and can cope more easily, but multiple losses take their toll on even the most resilient. Is it any wonder that some older people become irritable, controlling, depressed, reclusive, and/or develop behavior problems that baffle their families and caregivers? Next we discuss disenfranchised losses, and later chapters will speak of ways in which some of the grief and resulting depression can be addressed.

CHAPTER 4

Understanding the Disenfranchised Losses

SOME LOSSES DO NOT ELICIT a lot of support from family and friends. We call these losses "disenfranchised," because the griever has to grieve alone for the most part, or in a very different private way, without some of the attention that other losses bring. Friends and even family may not recognize these losses; even if they do, they can be uncomfortable and not know what to say or do, so they say or do nothing, leaving the griever without validation or social support.

The term "disenfranchised grief" was coined by Dr. Kenneth Doka, a leader in the field of grief theory and therapy, who published *Disenfranchised Grief: Recognizing Hidden Sorrow* in 1989. Until then, many had no name for the griefs they suffered, because they did not seem to be validated by others and had to be grieved alone, sometimes in secret.

Remember we defined bereavement as the loss of something important or valuable to us, which can include a loss by death, but is not necessarily limited to death. Separation from valued attachments to people, pets, possessions, familiar environments, and whatever represents an emotional attachment can trigger the grief response. Some of these griefs will sound familiar from preceding chapters. It is difficult to lump grief into a single category. You may run into some familiar kinds of grief in this chapter on disenfranchised grief. The categories are but different ways of perceiving grief, as if looking at the same grief from a different perspective.

There are many examples of disenfranchised grief, including:

Abortion

Abortion is considered a private matter. Women who have abortions are usually very private about them, choosing instead to live with the consequences in their own way, in silence. Sometimes family members know, but often they are not supportive of the decision, causing the woman to feel even more isolated in her grief.

Dr. Kenneth J. Doka, mentioned earlier in this chapter, a professor at The College of New Rochelle in New Rochelle, NY, wrote that "elective abortion is a prime example of disenfranchised grief. In fact, the polarized political atmosphere surrounding abortion is often a disenfranchising factor. Those who are pro-choice may invalidate any subsequent grief, while those on the pro-life side may acknowledge the loss, but in a very judgmental way." He goes on to say that not every woman who has an abortion experiences grief, but research indicates some women do. In his grief work with clients, he asks every woman whether she has experienced abortions, stillbirths, or miscarriages. We think of abortions affecting only women, but often men also carry guilt and grief over the destruction of a child they fathered.

Trudy Johnson, a therapist in Colorado, in her book, *C.P.R., Choice Processing and Resolution: Facing Grief After Abortion Without Fear*, tells the story of one of her clients who was in her late 90s, and who had voluntarily terminated a pregnancy in her 30s. She finally was able to tell the story of the secret she had been keeping for over 60 years, and seemed relieved to be able to weep and share her secret before she died.

A number of my clients have shared with me that they had abortions, some early in life, but some later in life as well. All but one of them admitted intense grief at the loss of the child, whether the pregnancy termination was legal or illegal, whether the client was married at the time or single, whether there was guilt or none, and whether it was because of a defect detected early in the pregnancy, or whether it was for convenience (or perceived convenience) at the time. The physical abortion itself does not seem to be the issue – and not the judgment from others who might know about it – but simply the grief associated with knowing there was a child who was not allowed to grow up, and the continued longing for that child. The reason for the decision and the opinion of others are quite separate from the grief issue, and I have discovered deep, life-long grief in older women.

Stillbirth

Because many feel there was no time to form a bond with a stillborn infant, this grief is often dismissed. One nurse attending a stillbirth insensitively told the parents, "Don't name this child. Save the name for a living child."

To have anticipated the birth of a child and made plans for its future, its room, its bed, and its clothing, is often discounted by people other than close relatives. Having to go home to face the empty room and the loss of dreams for that child are things parents have to grieve alone or with very little support. Many people feel that to give condolences and sympathy and to allow time to grieve seem to be reminding the parents of the event, when they could be moving forward and planning another pregnancy.

When I inquire of clients, either women or couples, whether they have children, and if so, how many, some respond with "two (or the number), but we had one son (or daughter, or baby) that was stillborn." The grief of an unfulfilled dream for a child that was anticipated but did not live does not go away with the birth of other children. No child can take another child's place, and the stillborn child is always grieved by the parents.

Related in some ways to stillbirth are babies who are born alive but live only a few hours or days. One friend said of her daughter who was born with an internal physical defect and lived only an hour, "She was so beautiful. I held her little body and tried to imagine what she would have grown up to be. I will love her and miss her the rest of my life."

These were her feelings, although family members were dismissing her grief over such a short life and encouraging her to "move on" and get on with her life.

Miscarriage

If stillbirths and very short lives at birth are not accorded acknowledgement and the parents are not given the right to grieve, miscarriages are often cavalierly dismissed with the words, "Well, you can try again," or "You can have another baby." Even well-meaning people say these words, and I am ashamed and embarrassed to admit that I have said them when I was younger and did not have the knowledge in the grief field I have acquired since then. I'm sure the words hurt the recipients, but certainly it was not intentional, and I hope this paragraph on disenfranchised grief and miscarriage can inform the reader of the inappropriateness of such comments. A miscarriage ends the hope for that child and the anticipation of joy that a child brings, and must be grieved, not dismissed.

Infertility

Common statements to parents who face this sadness are, "Well, you can always adopt," or "Have you tried [fill in the blank]?" (when the couple has tried everything known to medical science). The situation of infertility affects people in different ways, but if having biological children is something a couple has always dreamed of, this verdict represents a real loss, and the grief may extend into later adulthood and remain unacknowledged by others.

Death of Parent or Sibling in Childhood

Many people feel a young child is incapable of understanding the death of a parent or sibling, but the loss lingers with the child for a lifetime. Even if the surviving parent remarries, and even if the child has other siblings, these losses at a young age can affect a person through-out life.

Children are not often accorded enough grief support, because people feel they do not grieve as deeply as adults, do not really understand the loss, and that they will "get over it." Because children cannot grasp all the complexities of grief, they sometimes feel that their getting mad at a parent or sibling, or even wishing them gone, caused the parent or sibling to die and leave them abandoned. The effects of feelings of guilt and perceived abandonment make it more difficult for the child, when she grows up, to develop the trust necessary to achieve deep and satisfying relationships.

Author Judith Viorst, in *Necessary Losses*, reporting findings from The Institute of Medicine, states, "And the younger do worse than the older – studies find that one frequent consequence of childhood loss is a higher risk of adult-life mental illness."

Jill Krementz, in her book, *How it Feels When a Parent Dies*, quotes a 9-year-old whose father was killed in an auto accident: "I don't talk about it too much. I talk to my mother and my brother, but I don't like to talk to other people because I don't want them to know about it. I don't want people to treat me differently." Because she feels people would "treat her differently," she prefers to grieve in silence. A good example of a child's version of a stigmatized or disenfranchised grief.

A child who loses a sibling often suffers a silent grief, because the comforting and sympathy of others are more often directed only toward the parents. Friends and family members overlook the grieving child and focus on the parents' grief. The child feels alone and abandoned. When I look back on the death of our younger daughter, I realize that no one comprehended the needs of our older daughter, who was still very young. My husband and I were consumed with dealing with our own grief and unable to give the attention and comfort our surviving daughter needed. We tried to go on with our lives afterward, tried to make things normal, when in fact, things were not normal. I'm sure our daughter, now grown with a family of her own, still bears the scars resulting from her disenfranchised little girl grief. I would do things differently today, but I didn't know then what I know today.

Death of a Grandchild

The grief of grandparents is often overlooked, and the focus is on the parents of the child, leaving the grandparents to grieve without a great deal of support. As said in an earlier chapter, they grieve not only for the grandchild, but for their own children, wishing they did not have to endure such pain and feeling helpless to make things better.

Death of Ex-spouse

Dealing with the deaths of ex-spouses can be complex. At one time they were much loved, only later to become exes. Regardless of the reason for the divorce or the length of time between the divorce and the death of an ex-spouse, feelings are triggered that often confuse the surviving ex and make accepting the news a process of ambivalence, coupled with a flood of memories. The family of the ex-spouse might have remained friendly with the surviving ex, yet acknowledgement of the survivor's grief may not be forthcoming.

Even if the surviving ex-spouse attends the service he is not customarily seated with the family and instead is left to cope with the loss alone. One son, whose recently deceased father had been divorced many years, told his sobbing mother, "I can't understand your problem. If you didn't love him anymore and left him, then why are you going on like this? It doesn't make sense!" Even the mother's son could not begin to understand the ambivalent feelings that were rampant in the mother's grief, and those feelings remained unacknowledged and disenfranchised.

Death of Same-sex Partner

Whether in a state in which same-sex marriage is legal, or a state in which it is not, sometimes the surviving partner is not recognized by the family or by the public as having the right to grieve. If it was not a legal relationship and was not accepted by the deceased's family, the surviving partner can be denied the right to participate in the planning of the last services and denied the right to choose whether his loved one will be buried or cremated. Sometimes he is even denied the right to sit with or be a part of the family group in the public service.

One lesbian survivor bought a home in another neighborhood after her partner of 34 years died. Soon after she moved in, the new neighbors asked her if she was married, since they had seen no male around. She replied openly that her partner of 34 years was a woman and that she had died recently. One neighbor remarked (without thinking, we hope), "Oh, I thought since you seemed to be alone, you might be a widow." In other words, widowhood was an acceptable role and would have merited sympathy, but being the survivor of a same-sex partnership was a stigmatized role. Little sympathy was extended to the woman, and in a few months the house was again for sale. When no one acknowledges or understands grief, it can be a lonely and painful existence.

Death of Ex-lover

Many ambivalent feelings arise for the survivor of the death of an ex-lover, even if the length of time with that person was brief, but especially if the relationship was longer. The surviving wife or lover at the time of the death, and perhaps even the family, might not remember the ex-lover and accord her no acknowledgement of a right to grieve. This is true in a male/female relationship, but also in a same-sex relationship.

Death of Illicit Lover

This is a touchy situation, as the deceased may have been married and having an affair at the time of death, and no one knew about it except the illicit lover. Even if the affair was over before the death, the survivor will have mixed feelings about the relationship and the associated grief. While the lover may often attend the funeral, his relationship to the deceased was not known, and his grief cannot be acknowledged. He is left alone with his memories and his grief.

Death of Friend

Friendships can be as close as relationships with family members, yet the death of a friend is often thought of as being "just the death of a friend," eliciting a lesser amount of sorrow than when family members die. Yet the ties to a friend may be even closer than to some family members, and can include not only social friendships, but employee and co-worker relationships. When you spend many hours a day working with people, they usually are an important part of your life.

The summer before I was in the sixth grade, my best friend died suddenly of bulbar polio. Because not much was known about what caused polio, I was not allowed to go to the funeral, and no one talked to me about the loss of my friend. I was supposed to bounce back and enter sixth grade without her and I did, but my eleven-year-old heart was heavy. I remember feeling that no one understood. I walked home alone from school for many weeks after school started that year, crying all the way.

I mentioned in another chapter that a close friend in graduate school died and how alone I felt at her funeral. I was not a part of the family, but I had felt like a sister, because she and I and our husbands had been together so much and had shared so many happy times. I just could not imagine she was gone. I think my husband understood better than anyone, but I'm sure he did not anticipate my occasional tears even years after her death.

One of my first husband's co-workers died while they were on a business trip. A group was to attend a business meeting one morning after working together into the night on a presentation for the meeting. They had finally decided it was as good as they could make it and had retired to their respective hotel rooms around midnight. They were to meet for an early breakfast before the meeting. My memory is foggy about the actual details, but a reasonably accurate account is that when the colleague failed to show up for breakfast, Paul went to the man's room, only to find paramedics wheeling a gurney out. The maid had knocked and gotten no response, so she had entered and found him sprawled lifeless in a chair. I believe the determination was a heart attack. For weeks and months Paul had periods of deep grief, having been one of the last ones to see and talk with the man, yet Paul's grief was mainly dismissed, and his periodic bouts of moodiness were not linked by others to his shock and grief over the death of a co-worker.

Death from HIV/AIDS

Death associated with HIV or AIDS is becoming less stigmatized, but formerly the victims were blamed for their own deaths for either engaging in unprotected sexual activity or for using infected drug needles, and families had to bear the brunt of hearing this from people and from the media. Believing the victims had behaved inappropriately led to less support from some family members and friends.

I recently heard of a woman who kept her son's AIDS diagnosis secret from even her family, saying simply that he died of pneumonia. Of course, the illness that takes many AIDS victims' lives is pneumonia, but she refused to acknowledge the AIDS, feeling that would stigmatize the death.

Death from Drug Overdose

Accidental drug overdoses are still stigmatized, and many family members and friends have a difficult time talking about the cause of death. Whether it was because of illegal use of drugs or overuse of prescription drugs, many are reluctant to reveal the cause. This leaves family members and friends to create fictitious reasons for the death and mourn the real cause by themselves.

Death from Murder

Deaths from murder are often graphically described in the media, and family and friends are shocked and numb and sometimes unable to offer support to those closest to the victim. These losses are so traumatic that friends and family do not know what to say to the bereaved. Most of us cannot imagine the shock and upheaval such a violent death brings to the survivors. Many friends and family members remain mute for fear of saying the wrong thing. Capture and conviction of the killer may bring some solace to the family, but so often the murderer is not found, leaving the family to mourn not only the loss of the victim, but the unsolved case itself and the lack of justice.

As mentioned in the foreword to this book, author Lois Duncan's 18-year-old daughter, Kaitlyn Arquette, was murdered in 1989, and her murderer has yet to be identified and brought to justice. I encourage you to read Lois' two books about Kait's death, *Who Killed My Daughter?* and *One to the Wolves: On the Trail of a Killer.* You just might be the one to give them the tip they need.

Death from Suicide

Unlike deaths from murder, instances of suicide are rarely described in the media unless the person is involved in a crime or is very famous. One boy was only two when he witnessed his father's death from a self-inflicted gunshot. Now grown, he has trouble forming relationships. He still remembers the scene vividly, and remembers how his mother told him after the funeral that he was "the man of the house now." Quite a responsibility to lay on a two-year-old, and one that distorted his role in the family and in society as he grew up. The family never spoke of the father's death again, leaving the boy to grieve in his child-like way with no support at all.

In their book *After Suicide Loss: Coping with Your Grief*, Bob Baugher and Jack Jordan, both Ph.D.s and both deeply involved in the field of grief education, described the effects of losing a loved one by suicide: "A suicide can undermine your sense of trust in others and your belief in your own competence, self-worth, and mastery over your life. For almost all survivors, it produces a sense of having been injured by life, a realization that others whom you love can nonetheless do things that break your heart and wound your soul." Losing a person by suicide changes a survivor forever. Baugher and Jordan maintain that the survivor may carry aspects of grief for the rest of his or her life.

Death of Pet

The death of a pet receives no mention in the media unless you are famous. For instance, former President George W. Bush's dog, Barney, died of lymphoma, and President Clinton's Buddy was hit by a car and killed. Both made the news. But less well known people who lose pets get little consolation from friends and family, and if they do get comfort, it is usually of a shorter duration. For some people, pets are like family members and require a much longer period of grief than friends and family feel is appropriate.

When we lived in Texas, my friend Sandra lost her beloved dog to kidney failure. Within a few hours, one of Sandra's friends from down the street came bursting into her living room with a bouquet of flowers, laughing and making a joke of "I'm bringing flowers to the bereaved." Instead of comfort, this insensitive act trivialized Sandra's loss and made her feel worse.

I see clients who have lost pets, and their grief is as real and as intense as if they had lost a human family member. They need to know their feelings are normal, but many times people make light of those feelings or dismiss them entirely.

Losing a service animal on which the person has come to depend may lend an additional intensity to grief. The bond that develops between the two is considered one of the closest human/animal relationships. In addition, the patient grieves the loss of help the animal provided, but also dreads the prospect of having to start over with another animal and becoming accustomed to and bonded with it.

Divorce

The notices in the newspaper (if there are any) are brief and official-sounding in the case of divorce. Friends are often unsure of their allegiance in the case of divorce, whether they should support the husband or the wife. It can be difficult to be supportive of both. Families sometimes take sides and make family get-togethers miserable for everyone concerned, even the children and grandchildren of the couple. These feelings can persist for years and cause grief that lasts a lifetime.

Family celebrations of birthdays, graduations, marriages, and new grandchildren, all bring triggers that reignite the old feelings. Many older people are now survivors of divorce, whether it was years ago, or whether it was more recent. Divorce often brings feelings of failure, with the realization that what seemed like "perfect love" at one time somehow deteriorated into a dissolved marriage.

I have had elderly clients who are still grieving a divorce that occurred when they were young. My own grandfather was divorced at a young age before he married my grandmother, and he had two little boys with his first wife. The wife took the boys and moved back to her parents' home in the South, and did not communicate with him. Travel in 1903 was very difficult, and he didn't have the time off work or the resources to make a trip from New Mexico to Georgia to try to find his sons. He grieved into old age about their being taken away, never knowing them as they grew up, and never knowing whether he had grandchildren by those boys. Rather than consoling him about this issue, family members were hesitant to bring it up, thinking it would upset him, essentially causing it to be a disenfranchised loss. He died at age 70, in 1939. Since then, I have done genealogy research on the internet and found that one of the sons died as a toddler and the other never married, but my grandfather had no way of knowing that before he died.

Separation from a Relationship

Separation information is usually not in the newspaper unless the people involved are celebrities. Like divorce, separation creates a situation people are reluctant to address. The separation may be temporary or permanent, and people who know the couple often do not want to get involved. Couples are surprised that their friends abandon them at such times, just when some support would be welcomed.

Separation from Pet

When an older person has to move into a retirement apartment, assisted living community, or nursing home, often he can no longer have his pet with him. The grief of having to be separated from the pet is very real. My uncle hired 24-hour help in his home at great expense, rather than have to move into a retirement community without his little poodle. Some people do not have this choice, and their feelings of grief at separation from their pets are overlooked.

Adoption, Both for Mother and Child

Grief pertaining to adoption has already been looked at in Chapter 1 from the perspective of the infant, but bears examining again from the perspective of the biological mother in the light of disenfranchised grief. When a woman feels she needs to relinquish a child for adoption for any reason, it leaves a hole in her heart, and most biological mothers never stop wondering how that child is, what he looks like, what she is doing, etc. No matter how many other children they give birth to, the ones who were given up for adoption stay in their minds and hearts. If it is an open adoption, there is sometimes the opportunity to communicate with and see the child periodically. If it is a closed adoption, as so many were in the past, there is a good chance that few knew about the pregnancy or birth. In the mid-1950s, young girls or women were whisked off to "Aunt Betty's" or "Aunt Barbara's" for a year or so as a supposed "educational experience." If no one but the immediate family knew about the child, the grief was contained and was not discussed. The young girl or woman was supposed to forget about it and go forward with her life. The truth is that the biological mother never forgot, but was denied the process of dealing with her grief. Some mothers later search for the child, but hesitate to interfere with the child's life with the adoptive parents. The child himself may search when he is old enough, but again, often hesitates to interfere with the biological parents' lives for fear of causing pain and exposing a "secret."

Separation from Child (Surrogate Parent)

In these days of *in vitro* fertilization, someone other than the biological mother may be contracted to carry the embryo to full term for the parents. It takes a very strong woman to do this – to carry an infant within her body for nine months, all the time knowing she will not be able to keep it, but must relinquish it to the parents at birth. To date, not many studies have been done on the impact of grief that the surrogate bears as a result of this arrangement, but it is likely that it leaves emotional scars that the surrogate is hesitant to reveal.

Separation from Caretaker (Foster Parent)

Foster parenting also takes certain caring people to do the job professionally without becoming too emotionally involved with the children they know are theirs only temporarily. When it is time for the child to be returned to her biological parents or to adoptive parents, the foster parents are thought to be able to say goodbye easily and move on. It is unusual for a caring foster parent to be able to say goodbye without some grief, but it is kept inside, because by showing grief the foster parent might be indicating she is not suited for the position. And some children who are treated kindly and lovingly by foster parents also develop a bond with the foster parents that causes a form of grief when they are parted. (I am not talking about the kinds of foster parents that make the news for being negligent or abusive, but the ones who put their hearts and souls into caring well for children in transition.)

Separation from Friends

This topic has also been covered somewhat in a previous chapter, but from the disenfranchised standpoint, not many family members or caregivers or new friends in a new environment are going to want to hear how much a patient misses friends from whom she has been separated. She is supposed to integrate cheerfully, make new friends willingly, and not think about such things.

Separation from Home

When the death of a spouse or an illness necessitates relocating from a home in which someone has lived many years, the grief reaction often occurs. Even though the new house or apartment may be nice, it does not take the place of the home that embodies many years of fond memories. The relocation may be seen as a smooth process by families, and not enough time is allowed for the relocated person to grieve the loss of their home.

Separation from Environment

This loss, which includes neighborhood, neighbors, familiar shopping, services, and places of worship, has been discussed in an earlier chapter, but is often overlooked as an important loss, not adequately supported or validated.

Separation from or Loss of Possessions

I have already discussed having to downsize possessions because of a necessary move, but we have not looked at the loss of possessions because of fire, flood, tornado, or theft. Loss from fire, flood, or tornado is one of the most devastating losses, as many years of memories and keepsakes are destroyed. People who are very sentimental will grieve these losses for the rest of their lives. Loss from theft is also traumatic, with the added elements of anger and fear impacting the grief. We see the news on television or the internet and read about these kinds of losses in the newspaper and magazines, and we quickly pass over the tremendous grief that is attached to losing such important items.

Separation from Parents (Abuse or Illness)

If children of any age are removed from their family of origin by authorities for any reason, the loss is traumatic. Even children who are removed from their parents because of abuse long to be with them. The parents, who are supposed to love the child more than anyone else does, represent a type of "love" that seems illogical, but which research shows nevertheless usually is important to the child. Children will endure a lot of abuse or neglect before they will willingly be separated from their parents. Somehow they see the parents as their security, even when objective observers see it is necessary for the children's well-being for them to be with kinder, more loving adults. Those in authority see removal as "rescuing," but children see removal as the crumbling of all they know. Ask any child who has ever been removed from his parents' care, and you will find the trauma was great and lasts a lifetime. The child is considered to be "rescued," and their bonds with the abusive parents are not understood or validated.

Removal from the home for months because of illness of a parent, even if the removal is temporary, leaves a feeling of abandonment that can affect the child's personality over a lifetime. Studies have shown that children have a difficult time transitioning back with the absent parent, having lost some trust in the permanence of the situation.

Separation from Child (Taken Away)

Any parents who have had their child or children removed from the home by the authorities carry the guilt and grief of separation for a long time. One client whose children were grown confessed to me that he was still suffering from having had his children taken from his home many years ago because of a live-in girlfriend who abused them. At the time, he opted to stay with the girlfriend and lose his children, and he had grieved his decision for thirty-four years, but could not bring himself to share the story with anyone, therefore grieving alone.

Separation from Sibling(s)

Children can be separated when adopted or placed in foster homes. A child may remember having siblings, but loses contact with them and grieves the loss.

Also family feuds happen, and sometimes siblings become estranged. Earlier I mentioned my maternal aunts, who did not speak for decades, and how they would avoid family gatherings if they thought the other would attend. The younger aunt played the organ at my first wedding, while the other sister did not attend. The older aunt attended my father's funeral, while the other did not.

One of them voiced intense sadness over the situation and tried to reconcile with her sister. The other sister demonstrated only anger. The rest of the family spoke of it as "the situation," and we still do not know the origin of the rift between them. They went to their graves without resolution. Not only did it cause sadness for one sister (and possibly for the other, although she would not admit it), but it caused confusion and heartache for the whole family. It was never labeled as "grief," but it certainly was a disenfranchised form of grief, and was not spoken about outside the family.

Dysfunctional Home

"What would you change in your past if you could?" I sometimes ask clients. Some say they would have liked to have a family that was loving, or a father who was not an alcoholic, or a mother who expressed affection, or parents who did not fight, or siblings who were not sources of pain, and the list goes on. Living in a dysfunctional home affects the way children adapt to the external world. Later in life they realize it did not have to be that way, and they grieve for the kind of family they never had.

Loss of Body Part

Whatever the reason for the absence of a body part, whether by amputation because of an injury or the effects of disease, or whether because of a birth defect, the missing part is grieved. In the case of amputation of a limb or extremity, phantom limb pain is well known and can occur in up to 85% of patients who undergo amputation. The pain feels as if the amputated limb is still attached to the body, although it may seem to the patient the limb is different in size than the original, or in a distorted position. The intermittent or constant pain associated with the lost body part is a reminder of what has been lost, and while the patient may complain of the pain, the patient is not usually helped through the grieving process for the lost limb.

One study showed that even after the amputation of other body parts, such as the breast, phantom pain can occur, but is often overlooked or not appreciated by those caring for the amputee. Besides the possible phantom pain after breast removal, the removal of a part that is representative of the patient's gender can affect her feeling of being "female" and cause grief because an aspect of the patient's perceived femininity has been lost.

Birth defects have occurred throughout history. When the drug Thalidomide was prescribed for nausea in pregnant women during the 1950s and 1960s, the years in which the effects of the drug on pregnant women was not yet known, many babies were born with missing or deformed limbs. One of my friends had a brother about four years old who had flipper-like appendages where his arms would have been. He had, of course, never known what it was like to have normal arms, but when my friend and I would sew or paint, he would comment, "I wish I had 'those' like yours, so I could do that." He grieved for the missing parts, but also for the abilities of which he was deprived. I do not know where he is now, but as an adult does he still grieve for "those"?

Disabilities

People with restrictions on their abilities learn early not to talk about them constantly, knowing that family members, friends, or caregivers tire quickly of such talk. The common response is, "Well, but you do have other abilities," or "At least you can still think [or fill in the blank with whatever abilities are intact]." This is little solace for someone who has lost an ability or abilities, say from a stroke, and is grieving that loss. Acknowledging the loss with, "I'm sure it is difficult to try to do without that ability [again, fill in the blank]," validates the patient's feeling of loss. Otherwise, he grieves alone, feeling that others consider him lucky just to be alive, failing to realize his grief over what has been lost.

Retirement

Much has already been said about retirement, but for purposes of disenfranchised grief, we'll mention that retirement is often anticipated and seen to be a time of relief, free time, and the opportunity to engage in other activities. When the retired person makes the transition and after a while begins to miss the co-workers and the feeling of doing productive work, her remarks are often treated lightly and not acknowledged as a grief reaction.

Unrecognized Achievements

Parents have dreams for their children. My grandparents' dream for their daughters was to find good husbands and produce children. Only one daughter did. Another daughter never married, but achieved recognition academically and professionally, earning a Ph.D., teaching in a university, and becoming a national officer in an academic association. In her later years she lamented, "Mother and Daddy never acknowledged my successes. To them, getting married and having children were the ultimate successes for a woman. I have always felt I failed to win their approval. They did not even acknowledge my achievement when I was awarded my doctorate."

Historical Trauma

Historical trauma affects significant populations. Loss, over generations, of land, language, culture, and essential ways of being, in addition to loss of family, friends, and community members, leaves a lasting impression and needs to be grieved and validated. Some examples of historical trauma in relatively recent United States history are the placement of American Indians on reservations, the enslavement of African Americans, and the removal of Japanese Americans to internment camps during World War II, as well as discrimination, harassment, and atrocities associated with these events. Countless other groups of people in the world have suffered historical trauma over the centuries. While a full discussion of historical trauma is beyond the scope of this book, it is an important experience of disenfranchised grief, which is rarely included in loss and grief resources.

Remember that disenfranchised losses are those that most people do not acknowledge as causing a grief reaction. Most people simply neither validate these losses nor think of them as losses that need and deserve to be grieved. In the next chapter, we'll see what effect multiple losses, including these disenfranchised losses, have when they accumulate in a person's life.

CHAPTER 5

Looking at Grief and Losses over Time

OVERVIEW OF THE GRIEF PROCESS

KNOWING THAT MANY PERSONS ARE better able to learn by visual means, or by analogy to something familiar, I'd like for you to picture a highway representing life. We move along this highway doing the things that we do, living normally. All at once we suffer a bereavement, and our route changes. Instead of traveling along this highway as usual, we face a detour. Some people try to avoid the detour as if nothing has happened, but when trying to travel the highway when it has been damaged in some way, they find their journey becomes fraught with many complications, some of them affecting their life course in unexpected and seemingly unrelated ways. When we take the grief detour before resuming our travels on the highway, we have an opportunity to process our grief response, experience feelings associated with the event, and take time to let our minds, bodies and emotions begin to learn new ways of coping with life after the loss. The detour is not a predetermined length nor is it meant to be traveled in the same way by every griever.

Well-meaning relatives or friends may try to enforce their own time table on the bereaved, but it is a detour that is a unique passage for each individual. We have all known people who say to a grieving person, "You should be over that by now," or "It's time you moved on," or "That happened years ago, and you shouldn't still be thinking about it." Those kinds of remarks may be said with the best of intentions, but are not in the least helpful. Whether it's been a month or several years or longer, until the grief has been processed and validated it will continue to affect the patient's functioning.

Can you picture the imaginary detour? A highway suddenly takes one onto a side road, diverts one around construction obstacles, then connects again with the original roadway so that the journey can be continued.

One of the first areas of the detour has to do with the initial shock of the loss. As if we have been robbed, we are likely to react with anger and denial that this is happening to us. "Why? Why me?" we ask.

Some of the physical symptoms may be numbness or tingling of the hands and feet; nausea; weakness; fatigue; trouble sleeping; pains in the legs, stomach, or other parts of the body; or a feeling of having a lead weight in the pit of the stomach. Some people may have trouble swallowing, shortness of breath, headache, change in appetite, either not wanting to eat (with accompanying weight loss) or wanting to eat more than normal (with accompanying weight gain), or desiring mainly one type of food – sweet, salty, etc., or the person may dream profusely about the loss. Many of these symptoms produce a depressed immune system, which can lead to illness if proper health precautions are not taken.

Some of the emotional symptoms, also depending upon the severity of the event, may be crying, irritability, anger, irrational mood swings, or guilt over real or imagined acts or omissions that the survivor feels might have prevented the loss. Expressions such as "If only I had..." or "If only they had..." surface to haunt the person. In most cases these feelings are unfounded, but during this phase that doesn't matter to the griever. Somehow she feels she could have, or should have, done something to prevent the loss, and torments herself with these thoughts and feelings.

In some instances there actually may be a sense of relief, even though the loss is significant, especially if there has been great suffering for the patient, either physical or mental, beforehand. A sense of betrayal toward someone we trusted can engender anger, which can be directed at a higher power or at an individual who might have caused or could have prevented the loss. Abandonment can be felt, a sense of isolation with the absence of what was precious. Life can seem unreal, like walking through a fog.

Mental symptoms include operating in a robot-like fashion, kind of on auto-pilot, but not being able to concentrate for any length of time, and having some impairment in making decisions. Cognitive impairment may not be noticed by the griever, but may be noticed by others.

Few people experience every one of these symptoms, but most people in similar circumstances experience a number of them. Although each experience of grief is unique, enough similarities exist to allow us to make some generalities in the description.

As we move through the detour, the symptoms change slightly. Often despair sets in and colors our life. We may still experience many of the same symptoms of the initial phase, but depression may take over. Physically the person may do a lot of sighing and experience sleep disturbances, fatigue, and restlessness. Emotionally, he may feel loneliness, isolation, anguish, agony, feelings of hopelessness and helplessness, and fear, along with continued anger, guilt, betrayal, and irritability. Dreams, either disturbing or comforting, may continue to occur. Things that were interesting before no longer seem interesting. Concentration may still be poor. He may still experience difficulty making decisions, indicating temporary cognitive impairment.

As we travel farther into the detour we may eventually reach a phase in which the physical, emotional, and cognitive symptoms subside somewhat, although they may still occur from time to time. Interest in former activities begins to return little by little. The loss is still felt, but memories may be compartmentalized into a mental and emotional segment of life so that the griever can begin to move on, realizing the loss was a detour and had to be taken, because the loss needed to be grieved, but realizing she still has a life to be lived.

This detour is not a progression that once traveled, is over. Rather, think of the detour as a pendulum that can swing back and forth between the beginnings and the later parts. Many things can cause the return of certain feelings – hearing a song, smelling an odor of a perfume or after-shave lotion, seeing a favorite item. These are called "triggers" and can, even for years afterward, remind the survivor of the loss and bring back familiar feelings. It is not unusual for the trigger to cause the survivor momentarily to experience a mild form of an earlier stage of the detour. Grievers are sometimes surprised by the intensity of the feelings aroused by a trigger, but this experience is common.

Life after a loss will never be exactly the same as before, because there will always be a missing element that can never be replaced. A simplistic analogy is that of working a jigsaw puzzle and finding a piece missing – the picture is incomplete and never as beautiful as it was before the piece was lost. There is no replacement for the missing piece. We put the pieces back into the box, and we do not spend time trying to make the picture perfect without the missing piece. Similarly, at some point we have to come to terms with the losses in our lives, realize that life will never be as it was before the losses, and develop coping skills.

It is my belief that we never "get over" an important loss, but we learn to cope with it and regain our own lives, so that joy can eventually again become a part of who we are. When grievers are urged to get over a loss, their feelings are not validated and are made to seem less important. When they are given opportunities to talk about the event and the memories, really listened to, and allowed to cry and grieve without being shamed, they feel supported. If their physical needs are attended and their health status is nurtured, maintained, or even improved by some exercise and by proper nutrition, and if their social needs are met in appropriate ways, they can be helped to begin to feel purpose in life again at their own pace. They should not be forced to do things they are not ready to do. Certain grief rituals may be meaningful, such as planting a tree in memory of the loved one, lighting a candle at holiday meals, or recounting fun memories of the person in a family gathering. With the help of some of these suggestions, the majority of people can learn to cope with most losses and move on.

Losses Over Time

Some losses cause a longer detour than others, simply because of the frequency with which they occur or the manner in which they occur. Many losses in a short period of time generally result in "compounded grief." Later in this chapter we will look at certain kinds of bereavements that result, for various reasons, in "complicated grief."

Compounded Grief

Losses begin early in life for some, continue to occur, and generally become more numerous with aging. Take a moment to list your own losses, from the first you can remember – perhaps a pet, or a grandparent, or a childhood neighborhood in which you had many friends. This exercise will help you see the various losses that occur throughout life.

When many occur very close together, we call it compounded grief. They often occur in rapid succession, so that a person does not have time to process and grieve one before another comes along. Often each of these has not been validated by other people or grieved sufficiently, and they are added to the many other losses that have occurred throughout an individual's lifetime. For example, imagine losses we have discussed that affect multiple other losses – the loss of a spouse might mean a difference in financial security, which necessitates a move to smaller quarters, which necessitates selling or giving away some possessions, a change of environment, and perhaps loss of a pet. A decline in health may mean decreased abilities, which might mean moving where help is available, which again may lead to many of the losses noted above.

My mother-in-law had a stroke when she was in her 70s, and we found it necessary to move her closer to us in another state. She had already lost her husband, a grandchild, her parents, numerous siblings, many friends, her hearing, and her ability to speak clearly. Now, with this move to a room in a retirement residence in a strange city, she had to leave her home of many years, had to give up many of her belongings, her friends in her city, her environment, her familiar medical providers, her church, her independence, and...well, by now you know how to make a list of losses. About all she gained in this move was our ability to make sure she had affection from us and the physical care she needed.

While she seemed to take much of this in her stride at first, I began to notice some changes in her. She had always been a pleasant person. She could still be pleasant, but would make comments that disturbed us, like "I don't know why I couldn't still live at home. Why did I have to move to this big city? Nothing here is familiar to me," or "All the people in this place are old." My husband and I were young, busy with small children, trying to make our own way in life plus see that she had appropriate care, and did not realize nor take time to acknowledge all she had given up.

I got a call from the manager of the retirement residence saying we needed to come and pick up my mother-in-law because of her behavior toward the staff. Nothing pleased her there, and she was sometimes inconsiderate both of staff and of other residents. That was the start of a series of no fewer than four moves to other retirement residences, without our realizing what was causing it. If we had been better educated about grief at that time, we might have realized she was overwhelmed with multiple losses in a relatively short time. As it was, we all thought she had become just a difficult person to please.

One of my elderly clients was rolled into my office in a wheelchair, accompanied by her daughter, who was obviously at her wit's end. The expression on the daughter's face spoke volumes. The mother was living with the daughter and her husband, and required a lot of physical care from an injury. The client had agreed to come to my office, but was resistant to counseling, and the family was pleading for my help.

The daughter gave me some background – her mother had lost her husband, had an accident, had been moved to the daughter's home, and was creating chaos. Both the daughter and her husband were worn out and irritable with the mother's continual demands.

I asked the daughter to leave the therapy room and sit in the waiting room for the rest of the session. That left the mother, tight-lipped and defiant, with arms folded, alone with me. She said, "I don't know what you can do for me. I'm just not worth much anymore." I engaged her in conversation and asked about her earlier life. It became evident she had done many things she was very proud of, but she said no one wanted to hear about them. She complained that her daughter and husband were too busy to listen to anything that had happened to her before the accident. She opened up to me and by the time the hour was over, she was even smiling occasionally. Our time up, I asked her if she was willing to come back, and she agreed to come back in three days. When I went out to get the daughter, who was prepared for the worst, she was ecstatic that her mother was willing to participate in therapy.

Over a few weeks, as we talked about her many losses throughout her life, this mother became more cheerful and pleasant, but it was still a drain on the daughter and son to provide all the care necessary. In a joint session with the three of them, I suggested that moving the mother to an assisted living apartment might be a possibility, though I had never made that suggestion to any of them before. The daughter frowned and said they had mentioned that to the mother, but she was adamantly against it. I was looking to see what facial expression the mother had at my suggestion. This time, to their surprise, the mother did not reject the idea. I told her she might like being a bit more independent and being around people her own age with whom she would have much in common. She kind of liked the idea of being away from them and in her own space, and asked if they played games there. I assured her that most assisted living communities have activities directors who arrange games and other fun things for the residents.

She was hooked. Someone had taken an interest in her as an intelligent, accomplished person, not as an invalid needing care. Someone had acknowledged her losses. She asked for her family's help, and within a couple of weeks of our joint session, she had moved into her own small apartment in a well-run assisted living community.

After I felt she was settled into her new environment, I went to visit her and asked her if she wanted to come back to my office for more therapy. She replied, "No, I don't think I need to. I'm pretty happy here, and they are taking good care of me. I like the people at my dinner table. My daughter comes to visit, and sometimes they take me out to dinner with them. I have plenty of time here to read and watch TV, and when I want to be with other people, I go to the activities room and see what's going on. Thank you for your help, but I think I'm doing okay." Later the daughter called to thank me for giving her and her husband their lives back.

Now I'm no magician, and some stories don't end so happily, but frequently family members, friends, and caregivers wonder why there are changes in attitude and/or behavior, and sometimes it's just that no one has taken the time to acknowledge and validate all the grief that has piled up in someone's life. Each grief needs to be acknowledged and processed.

Complicated Grief

Special kinds of losses result in complicated grief, because of various circumstances surrounding the event. We will look at a few.

Losses that do not result in death, but which require more intense adjustments, are those that affect a person's capabilities. If a painter cannot use his arms or hands, a part of his identity is lost, as well as a functional body system. If a dancer cannot use her legs or feet, a part of her identity is lost. The same is true of a singer who loses the use of her voice, a runner who can no longer run, or anyone who is talented but who no longer has the means to utilize a special talent or enjoyable avocation. These kinds of losses have a great impact and make adjusting to the grief more complicated.

Losses associated with death are made more complicated by special circumstances surrounding the death. Sudden unanticipated death, such as from a stroke, heart attack, accident, suicide, or murder, does not provide the survivors a chance to say goodbye. This inability leaves them with unsaid messages they wish they could have conveyed to the deceased. They long to be able to "go back" and say some last words to the person, but are unable to do so. They grieve this situation along with the actual death.

If circumstances prevent survivors' being able to view the body, there is a lack of closure and a difficult adjustment to the reality that the death has occurred. Funerals with the body present are one way to provide a form of closure for survivors, as well as private viewings if preferred, and even though it is sometimes difficult to see the deceased lifeless and cold, it is an imprint on dazed and confused survivors' minds that helps them acknowledge the reality of the death.

Sometimes the reason for the inability to view the body is because of the distance to be traveled or the health of the survivor, but sometimes it is because the body is never recovered. An historic example is the sinking of the Titanic in 1912, a disaster in which only 337 bodies of the over 1500 victims were found, or roughly only one in five. Another example in our recent past is the destruction of the Twin Towers in New York in 2001, by terrorists' taking over airliners and crashing into the buildings. The number of people killed in that attack is believed to be over 2500, but no trace of the bodies or body parts has been identified for about half of those listed as deceased. Less than 300 bodies were found intact, and only twelve of them could be identified by sight, leaving many families with no visible remains on which to focus their grief. Other examples abound: Missing in action in the service; natural disasters such as tsunamis, tornados, earthquakes, and volcanoes; and human-caused disasters such as plane crashes, kidnappings, and other examples you may think of that I have omitted. The point is that if there is no recovery of the remains, with no chance to view them, the grief process is often complicated.

A term coined in the 1970s by Pauline Boss, Ph.D., is "ambiguous loss," referring to the propensity of survivors to wonder whether the person somehow escaped death and may be living after all. Not having remains leaves the question open to survivors, in spite of circumstantial evidence that may point to the likelihood that the person is dead.

Felicia Fonseca writes about two planes that crashed over the Grand Canyon in 1956, and some of the victims' remains never were identified. One woman was four years old when the accident occurred, and her father was a passenger on one of the planes. The little girl was told her father was on a business trip and would be back soon. She eventually stopped asking her mother when. She said the trauma runs deep, but she can talk about the crash more openly now. One man, whose father was on one of the planes, was 12 when the crash occurred. "I used to think every night that my father would walk out of the Grand Canyon, sunburned and scraggly, saying, 'They screwed up, I'm fine, here I am,'" the son said. The uncertainty and not knowing is one of the cruelest types of grief. The brain does not deal well with ambiguity.

Another cause of death that will likely cause complications is an accident in which someone can be blamed (such as an auto accident in which a driver was under the influence of alcohol or other drugs or was talking or texting on a cell phone, or perhaps an industrial accident in which a fellow worker was negligent). These kinds of accidents are often complicated by a great deal more anger than occurs in a natural death, because there is a specific focus for the anger, often including another living individual.

Suicide almost always creates a complicated grief pattern because of the feelings of betrayal, anger, failure, guilt, and helplessness with which survivors deal after such an event. Betrayal because perhaps the person who died had promised he would never kill himself, anger because he did not say goodbye and left so suddenly without talking about his problems, failure and guilt because most of those bereaved by suicide feel they could have (or should have) done something to prevent it, and helplessness because they could not prevent it and don't know how to cope with the aftermath and questions that can never be answered.

Instances of murder engender many of the same traumatic, complicated feelings that suicide creates, with some important differences. There is tremendous anger toward the perpetrator(s); the sadness over failure to be able to say goodbye to the victim; trauma at having to identify the victim in gruesome circumstances; sometimes guilt because, like suicide, the bereaved feel they should have or could have (or wish they could have) done something to prevent this catastrophe; and helplessness because they could not prevent it, have to deal with the aftermath of dealing with the police and the legal system, and often feel intruded upon and at the mercy of these supposed helpers. This grief is further complicated in cases in which the killer is not found quickly – sometimes the killer is not found at all, leaving unresolved loose ends hanging on the edges of this most horrific crime.

Other instances of complicated grief include many of the examples of disenfranchised grief discussed in Chapter 4, such as an abortion or the death of an illicit lover. The reason some of those are classified as complicated is that the person feels unable to acknowledge the source of grief publicly and usually must deal with it alone.

The grieving process is never without struggles. Obviously, any of these compounded or complicated griefs (and sometimes there are cases of both compounded *and* complicated kinds) mixed in with more griefs over a lifetime can cause the bereaved to have greater difficulty navigating the detour described at the beginning of this chapter and cause them to require more time to progress through the detour.

It is important to alert caregivers and families to the complex effects of bereavement in its many forms and perhaps help them acknowledge and deal more effectively with grieving people, especially older persons with many years of losses. Ideally, grief demands acknowledgement. Acknowledgement by others validates the feelings of the person and lets her know she is not grieving in total isolation. In the next chapter we will look at ways to identify grievers, notice depression, and help make life more enjoyable for them.

CHAPTER 6

Helping Optimize Patients' Health

DEPRESSION IS NOT A NORMAL part of aging. Many times grief leads to depression. Sometimes the depression is relatively short-lived, as is usual in a single episode of grief, but when losses are many, depression can set in for a long stay and be noticed by others. Some signs of depression can be:

Slowness of movement, absent any physical cause.
Stooped posture, absent any physical cause.
Lack of interest in things that were formerly interesting.
Lack of interest in appearance and grooming, if normally well-groomed.
Cynical or pessimistic statements about life.
Periods of crying.
Failure to engage with others.
Sleeping more than usual, or less than usual.
Either decreased or increased appetite.
Irritability.

The caregiver's task is to help make life as enjoyable as possible for the patient. With that in mind, we will look at some things that can help.

Optimizing Physical Health

Regular Checkups

Making and keeping regular appointments with a patient's physician are essential, plus extra appointments when situations call for them. Only by staying in control of health issues like blood pressure, cholesterol, and blood sugar, can one enjoy the optimal level of health that will make life more enjoyable. Caregivers can make notes between doctor visits and be prepared to report symptoms or changes that seem unusual. Signs of depression should be mentioned to the physician, and she may want to prescribe antidepressants, recommend dietary and exercise modifications, and/or recommend counseling.

Exercise and Movement

Exercise and movement appropriate for the physical condition can have beneficial effects. Pilates, yoga, light weight lifting, Tai Chi, aqua aerobics/swimming, and walking have each been shown to slow the effects of stress and aging and aid in maintaining flexibility. Exercise and movement can improve the quality of life by decreasing body fat, boosting muscle strength, and improving cardiovascular health, balance, and mobility. If mobility is limited, exercise and movement in a sitting position can still be beneficial. Exercise and movement help our brains as well, by producing endorphins, which have a calming effect and can help in controlling depression.

Nutrition and Hydration

Proper eating and drinking are important. We never outgrow our need for proper, balanced, healthy nutrition. Drinking water and other healthy liquids helps keep our bodies hydrated.

Mary J. Lemm Davis, M.S., Registered Dietitian, and Licensed Dietitian, contributes helpful information for families and other caregivers (Personal communication, Mary J. Lemm Davis, October 4, 2013). Davis says, "Body weight may change with age. Being overweight increases the risk for chronic diseases, but being underweight may not allow the body to fight against diseases and premature death."

Malnutrition must be prevented, to ensure the best health possible. Changes in the gastrointestinal tract may affect how nutrients are absorbed. According to Davis, even though with each decade of life caloric needs decrease about five percent due to declining physical exercise and changes in the body's metabolic rate, the same nutrients are still needed.

Taste and smell may become less sensitive with age, resulting in reduction in appetite. Care should be taken to see that issues such as ill-fitting dentures, loss of teeth, or the onset of gum disease don't contribute to malnutrition. Some people may have trouble swallowing, especially after a stroke, and sometimes an evaluation by a professional is needed.

Davis continues, "With aging, people may not feel as thirsty, so dehydration is a real risk. Older adults need to drink a minimum of six cups of water or fluids each day." The author knows from my experience working in nursing homes, it is often necessary also to monitor fluid output and report findings to the patient's physician, especially with dementia patients, because fluid intake is a challenge. Dementia patients often forget to drink or don't remember how much they have had. Urinary tract infections (UTIs) are common for this reason.

"Constipation can be a problem because of medications or a decline in activity," cautions Davis. "Three to four servings of both fruits and vegetables will provide fiber to help prevent the problem. Use freshly-prepared foods as often as possible to avoid the sodium (salt) content of many purchased or pre-prepared foods. Patients concerned about cholesterol can include the following in their diet – egg whites; low-fat dairy products; oils such as olive oil, canola oil, and peanut oil; and nuts and seeds."

A *New York Times* article in 2011 announced that Michelle Obama, Agriculture Secretary Tom Vilsack, and Dr. Regina M. Benjamin, Surgeon General, had replaced the former Food Pyramid with a new visual representation called MyPlate. Imagine a plate split into four sections – fruits, vegetables, protein, and grains. Government sources elaborate on the plan – recommendations include making about half the plate vegetables and fruits, then about a third of the plate grains and the remaining part protein. In the diagram of MyPlate, a small circle beside the plate represents dairy products, such as milk or yogurt. This is often a simple way to ensure all the nutritional needs are met, but the recommendations from Davis about sodium and cholesterol also need to be taken into consideration.

Davis says, "Nutrient supplements are not needed when a wide variety of foods are chosen and can be safely eaten. Having a dietary assessment done by a registered dietitian with a referral by the patient's health care professional may be helpful for many aging individuals and/or their caregivers who have dietary concerns."

Optimizing Emotional and Mental Health

Listening to Their Stories

One of the things older people miss is having someone who will take time to listen to their stories. Most have had very interesting lives and are eager for those around them to know about things they have done. Spending a little extra time each day just listening can be rewarding for both the caregiver and the patient.

When my mother-in-law had a stroke with accompanying aphasia (inability to speak or speak clearly), the caregivers in her nursing home seemed to have no time to try to decipher what she was trying to say. This was very frustrating for her, and emphasized yet another loss to her – the loss of ability to communicate even her basic needs. When I visited her, I allowed enough time to sit patiently and let her talk. I would guess at some of the words she was trying to say, and when I guessed correctly, her eyes shone with delight. I gradually learned to understand her fairly well, but it took time and patience. I was determined to "hear" her, and her appreciation was reward enough. This was a specific instance of listening under unusually difficult circumstances, but often listening requires only time and interest.

If the patient can speak into a recorder, someone can transcribe the stories and have them bound into a book. Having recorded this for his family and posterity gives him the realization that his life has meaning for future generations. I have seen this process help repair sibling relationships and revive shared history, as well as serve as a connection with younger generations.

When my mother was in her late 70s, I was embroiled in the life story project (more fully described in the next chapter), so on one visit I took my tape recorder and asked her some questions about her childhood and early life. We filled two one-hour tapes, and I transcribed them for her grandchildren. They had no idea that when she was two years old she wandered away from her yard, and a neighbor found her walking on the railroad track and took her home. They also were unaware that her father planted 20 pecan trees around their property and gave the five children the chore of daily carrying water in buckets to each tree. With a faraway look as if reliving the actual event, she said, "Those buckets were *so* heavy!" What a treasure her stories are – not only for our family now, but for the satisfaction and importance she felt when sharing those stories for her grandchildren and great-grandchildren to read.

Author Lois Duncan tells about taping her elderly mother-in-law's account of her life as a farm woman raising five sons during the depression. "It contained incidents that even my husband knew nothing about. After her death I printed copies and had them distributed at a family reunion. The younger generation was fascinated by the stories about the girlhood of a great-grandmother they'd known only as 'Nana'." (Personal communication, Lois Duncan, October 9, 2013)

Validating Their Feelings

"Oh, don't feel that way!" How many times have you heard that from someone or said that to someone? By telling someone not to feel a certain way, you are dismissing her feelings as unimportant.

Feelings are important, and people can learn to cope with their feelings if they are acknowledged and validated by those around them. If a patient feels sad, acknowledge the feeling and ask what is causing the sadness. If she is angry, acknowledge the anger and let her speak about it. Just knowing someone cares about the feelings is often enough to lessen the impact of the mood. An understanding ear can go a long way toward helping people feel someone cares.

Valuing Their Possessions

Always respect their possessions. Take time to let them tell you any stories associated with their valued items. These are the possessions they have chosen to have near them, and we can assume these things have meaning for them. Remember the list you were instructed to make in Chapter 3 – the meaningful things you would want to take with you if you had to move to limited quarters? These are the items we are talking about – the ones most important to the person.

Sentimental attachment to their belongings can be very important to them. One woman in an assisted living community had a collection of dolls. Some were well-preserved, but some were dirty and worn. A well-meaning caregiver, trying to help the woman downsize her belongings to fit into a smaller area, suggested she keep only the nicer-looking dolls. The woman was incensed. She said, "The worn ones are the most precious, because they remind me of my favorite memories. I can remember getting them, sleeping with them, and playing with them with my sisters. Those would be the last to go!"

A gentleman in a nursing home requested that his family bring in his rod and reel and place them on a shelf where he could see them. One of the housekeepers came in to clean and placed them out of his sight. He became agitated and called for help. When a caregiver came into his room, he said, "I look at my rod and reel and remember the first fish I ever caught, at age four, and the biggest trout I ever caught in my life, and all the times I went fishing with my granddad, dad, and later my sons. That rod and reel represent a big part of my life, and I want to be able to see them."

Respecting Their Privacy

Always knock before entering their rooms, even if they are unable to respond. The knock lets them know you respect their privacy and their space. One of the things they have given up is privacy, especially if they need a great deal of help with bathing, grooming, and/or toileting. Help them retain a part of their dignity.

Providing Choices

Things as simple as asking a patient how she would like to be addressed gives her an important choice. Some people do not mind being called by their first name, but others would rather be called by their title and last name, as "Mrs. Jones," or "Mr. Smith."

One woman, when going to a new physician's office for her appointment, spoke to the physician about the way the nurse had called her into the room for her appointment. She had been addressed by her first name, and it offended her. She said, "I've been married 65 years, and I go by Mrs. Edwards. Only family and very close friends call me by my first name." It is a simple thing to ask someone what she would like to be called. I hope the physician trained his nurse to address a new patient by her formal name, then later ask what she would prefer to be called.

Other simple choices are asking what a person would like to eat, if there are two choices, or asking him what he would like to wear, giving him a couple of choices. This has been discussed in another chapter, but having some choices in life, and the ability to make decisions, no matter how small, can be important to someone who has little control in his life.

Rituals

For individuals and groups, commemorating the dates of special events concerning loved ones who have died can be comforting and helpful in acknowledging the grief. Birthdays, anniversaries, and death dates can be kept in a card file and mentioned near the dates. Something as simple as a card or note, or perhaps even a single flower given at these times, can let an individual know you remembered.

For groups, it is appropriate to have a small memorial ceremony once or twice a year to acknowledge the special dates of loved ones lost. Reading a list of names of group members or close relatives with birthdays, anniversaries, and death dates can be incorporated into a simple ceremony with lighted candles. Sometimes a professional, such as a pastor, counselor, or hospice worker can be recruited to lead this short ceremony. It is comforting for many people to know their loved ones are not forgotten.

Perhaps at the end of the ceremony even a mention of "unspoken birthdays, anniversaries, and death dates," as in the case of disenfranchised griefs, can be a healing balm for those carrying hidden losses. The "secret losses" can be heavy burdens to bear.

Teaching Forgiveness

Holding grudges, carrying "baggage" of old hurts, and hating does not do a thing to the person against whom the grudge is held. The person it hurts is the one who holds it. What is done is done and cannot be undone, and life is too short to spend time and energy holding a grudge. Some repetition of this view of grudges can help to convince people that holding a grudge is useless and a waste of effort. Sometimes I find a client is holding a grudge against someone who is dead!

Small books with short readings on forgiveness are available and can be helpful to use with either a group or an individual. Letting "times you've been wronged" take up space in your head is hurtful to you, so I suggest to people that they "evict" the grudge and use the vacated space for happy, optimistic thoughts. Forgiveness is not a gift you give someone else. It is a gift you give *yourself.*

Encouraging Gratitude

Gratitude can be cultivated. There are many books that focus on gratitude, some with daily readings. Emphasizing the things for which we are thankful can redirect the mindset from sadness and depression to gratitude. Beginning a day with gratitude can set the tone for the whole day.

This is not a "mind over matter" experience – it is building new neural pathways in the brain, a learning experience. Even if some things are missing from life, we can learn to be thankful for the things we still have. My first husband, Paul, while battling leukemia, never lost his sense of gratitude. One of his favorite sayings was, "Any day you wake up breathing is a good day!"

Everyone can be encouraged to name one thing each day for which they are thankful. It can be as something as simple as seeing a beautiful sunrise, receiving a letter in the mail (bills or junk mail don't count, unless one is grateful for such things), stroking a pet, or hearing a beautiful song. In groups, each person in the group can be asked to name one thing that has happened that day for which he is thankful, and it can't be something that someone else has already named. After all, they are all breathing, so it has to be something besides that.

Patients can be encouraged to write in a journal, naming three things they are grateful for that day. They go to bed feeling appreciative for the good things that happened that day, full of thankfulness and gratitude, which in turn, produces more good feelings the next day.

Emphasizing New Roles

Our roles change as time goes by. A discussion on how roles change can spark ideas about current roles. People can name roles they've filled at different times in their lives – child, wife, father, teacher, student, manager, nurse, contractor, etc. They can be helped to see that the role they have now is also significant – wise elder, friend, cheerful relative, father, mother, grandparent, uncle, aunt, etc. One of my clients, when asked, "Who is the person most important in your life, and why?" said, "My uncle, because he taught me to fish, and he really listened to me. He showed me respect."

Elders need to realize they still have tremendous influence on younger people. They can be role models young people will remember as they grow in maturity.

Compassionately taking care of the physical, emotional, and mental needs of a patient will go a long way toward helping her learn to cope with the cumulative griefs of life. Fortunate is the individual whose caregiver cares enough to attend to these aspects. The next chapter is filled with suggestions for activities that can enrich an older person's life and teach healthy ways of coping.

CHAPTER 7

Providing Enjoyable Activities

STRUCTURED ACTIVITIES CAN BE FUN and uplifting, whether done with an individual or with a group. Currently, there are about three women for every two men age 65 or older. The tendency will be to gear activities and attention to things interesting mainly to women, but remember that in a group, many activities can be enjoyable for both men and women.

In one retirement community the activities director started a group for people who liked to do sewing handwork – knitting, embroidering, crocheting, or tatting, whatever appealed to the residents there, and perhaps types of sewing at which they were skilled. The level could be very basic, as making potholders on a plastic loom to give as gifts or to sell at the annual craft bazaar, or as complex as a resident's working on a counted cross stitch project or knitting a sweater. While the activities director expected all of the participants in the group to be women, to her surprise, a male resident showed up and was quite an accomplished knitter!

The same situation occurred in reverse, when she organized a fishing trip to a small lake nearby. She expected the ones who signed up to be men, but several women said they also loved to fish, and the whole mixed group enjoyed the outing.

Encourage them to participate in activities they haven't tried. If an elder has a talent she can share, encourage her to be a teacher to others. MJ Harden, in a book on Hawai'ian elders, writes about Elizabeth

Lee, a weaver of hats, who felt she was a "nobody" at one time. She was encouraged to teach her weaving skills to younger people, and she said, "I'm thankful that I could share this knowledge. I didn't realize it was something important until now." There are probably many seniors who can enjoy teaching a valuable new skill to others.

We get into habits that are comfortable, but trying new things helps change our habits and get the neurons in our brains firing in a different way. Author Tara Bennett-Goleman tells about a gerontologist she knows who says, "One of the biggest problems people have as they age is 'psychoschlerosis' – hardening of the attitudes!"

Changing Attitudes with Mindfulness

When we change some habits, our attitudes change. Try asking seniors to write a sentence or two with their non-dominant hand. This sounds like a strange way to break a habit, but having to focus and think about how to draw the letters will draw on neurons that haven't been used. They may even be surprised at what the hand is led to write. As most of you probably know, the right side of the brain is thought of as the emotional, artistic, musical, creative side, and the left side is thought of as the analytical, detail-oriented, mathematical and language side. The right side of our body is controlled mainly by the left side of the brain, and the left side of our body is controlled mainly by the right side of our brain. In cases of stroke or accidents in which the brain is damaged, the brain can often do an amazing job of learning to do the work of the other side, but that is a laborious task and takes time. The original design was, as I have said – right brain, left side of body; left brain, right side of body.

Left-handed people who try writing with their right hands are often surprised at the matter-of-fact sentences they write from the analytical left side of the brain, and right-handed people who try writing with their left hands can be surprised at the emotion that is shown by exercising the artistic-emotional right side of the brain. Reading the products of this exercise aloud, either to a family member, caregiver, or to a participating group, can be a fun and sometimes laughable experience.

Another fun mindfulness exercise (think of mindfulness as "awareness" or "focusing.") is to ask a patient (or a group) to fold his arms in front the way he always does, the way that is comfortable and habitual. Then ask him to change and fold them in the opposite way. There will likely be some confusion (and perhaps some laughter) as he tries to decide which arm goes where, and there will be some discomfort with that way, because even though we just reverse the procedure, habit tells us there is a "correct" way to fold our arms.

Remembering that mindfulness is a form of focusing or becoming aware, try naming a color and having the patient find and point out all the things in the room that are that color. We are so accustomed to seeing the view of the room as a whole, that when we break it down into individual items of one color, we notice things we hadn't noticed before. I have done that exercise with clients who say, "Oh, I never had looked at that chair closely to see all the colors that are there." One client, whom I had been teaching about mindfulness, came into my waiting room at her appointment time, but stood staring at the floor. I thought that odd, and I looked to see if something was wrong. She said, "You have a new rug." I responded, "No, that is the same rug I have had there for years. You are just beginning to be more aware of your surroundings."

Mindfulness can have a calming and soothing effect. Have the person close her eyes and concentrate on her breath. The only focus is on the breath. Slowly, in a calm voice, instruct her to brush aside all distracting thoughts. A simple mantra while breathing slowly is, "Breathe in serenity" (as she inhales), and "Breathe out anxiety" (as she exhales), repeated for several breaths. This can be helpful to a patient who is anxious.

There are many kinds of mindfulness exercises. Have someone settle into a comfortable position, become very relaxed, close his eyes, and begin to listen to the sounds he hears – perhaps a clock ticking, a fan whirring, a cat meowing, traffic driving past. Have him pay attention to the sounds he usually disregards as meaningless, or that he usually doesn't notice at all. In this same position, have him notice the feel of the chair or bed underneath his body and notice how it feels to be supported. Suggest he notice the fabric of his clothing or the bedding against his skin – is it smooth...silky...stiff...rough...flexible? Tell him to notice how it feels against his legs, arms, and torso. These sensations are usually overlooked, and becoming aware of the everyday things are lessons in mindfulness. Mindfulness can help people change their attitudes by forming new connections in the brain. Sometimes a new perspective on our environment can work wonders.

Gardening

Planting seeds and watching the sprouts come up, or planting plants and nurturing them and seeing them thrive and flower or produce edible vegetables or fruits can create interest in many people. Whether gardening in a group or individually, whether planting a few seeds in individual pots or planting a small garden, seeing the miracle of growth can be encouraging. For those persons for whom stooping or bending is not possible, raised flower beds can be constructed to allow them to reach the soil and plants easily. For those who are in their rooms a major portion of the time, plastic trays can hold several small pots of plants and be placed near a window.

In 1976, two researchers, Langer and Rodin, published a study in which one part dealt with gardening and the elderly. Their study was actually to see what effect control and responsibility would have on elderly residents, ages 65 to 90, of a nursing home. Two groups were selected. The members of one group of residents were given plants to care for – they could decide when and how much to water them, and the plants were their responsibility. The members of the second group of residents were also given plants, but these residents were told the nursing home staff would be responsible for watering and caring for the plants. There is much more to both the original study and the follow-up study done by Rodin and Langer in 1977.

For simplicity's sake and the relevance to this topic, the studies showed that giving the patients some appropriate responsibility and choices and a sense of control over certain things in their lives, including the care of the plants, caused them to be more engaged in life, and showed, in the follow-up study, that the participants even lived longer than those in the control group.

Gardening, whether planting a small garden or caring for house plants, is certainly worth trying with those who will become involved in such an activity. Nature itself often has a healing quality.

Movement and Musical Activities

Journalist Tammy Malgesini, in her article on providing musical activities for special needs groups in the Northwest, quotes a member of a musical group: "Music just speaks to people. It feeds your soul." Music has long been credited with "soothing the savage beast" or "soothing the soul."

Many activities can be programmed around music. Simply playing music and having people listen to their favorite tunes has a soothing quality. Having them sing along or participate by playing an instrument are even more interactive ways to engage them. Some retirement centers and assisted living communities invite residents to form choirs or instrumental groups. Activity directors often have youth or church choirs come to the communities and perform for residents, realizing music can raise spirits and modify moods.

I was an only granddaughter on my mother's side of the family, and my grandmother had been a concert pianist. Her father had given her an ornate piano when she was nine years old, which she kept all her life. As a child, I grew up sitting on the piano bench and listening to Nanny play. After I was old enough, I began to play, too, when we visited, and the song books available to me at Nanny's house contained the old time songs. I didn't know the difference, so I learned to play and sing "Aunt Dinah's Quilting Party," "By the Light of the Silvery Moon," "Smile a While and Give Your Face a Rest," and others I can't remember at the moment, most of which many of you have probably never heard. But you get the gist – I was going back a few generations in my musical learning, which stood me in good stead when I later began to work in a nursing home. The groups of residents loved it because the song leader knew all their favorites. How could I have known how handy *that* would be?

The outcome of my stint as song leader was that the residents looked forward to song time even more than Bingo, and if you work in an eldercare community, or if you've ever been closely associated with a resident of one, you know that Bingo is one of the highest-ranking activities among the residents. One activities director almost got ostracized by the residents because she dared to try to change the schedule and put Bingo on a different day. For song time to outrank Bingo seemed almost too good to be true, but it did. And they never seemed to get tired of singing the same old-time songs. Every once in a while I'd try teaching them a current popular tune, just for variety, and they would acquiesce, but then would ask for "In the Gloaming, Oh My Darling," or "School Days, School Days."

So, listening to music and singing seem to be beneficial. When you add some movement, as simple as swaying to the rhythm, or clapping to the rhythm, the music seems to have an even greater impact on enjoyment. Those who can get up and dance or move to the music report feeling a freedom that "makes me happy," in the words of one 77-year-old dancer. Even gentle movement to music when dancing, swaying, or clapping, can create endorphins that have a calming, yet invigorating effect.

Music in various forms, whether listening to upbeat instrumental or vocal numbers, or whether singing or adding swaying, clapping, or dancing, can be a creative outlet that can help patients who are carrying accumulated grief. It can also stimulate those with dementia to reminisce about their youth. For those who can hear, never underestimate the power of music.

Charades

Someone can write song titles, book titles, or movie titles from the 40s, 50s, and 60s on slips of paper and let a volunteer from the group pick one out of a container. The rules for charades can be as strict or as loose as the leader chooses to be appropriate for the group, but the object is to act out the title that is picked – without saying a word. Members of the group guess the words and finally put them together to call out the title. This can also be played in teams, with several people acting it out at the same time and the other members of the group guessing.

Show and Tell

Remember "show and tell" time in kindergarten and the early grades? How fun it was to bring something from home and tell the class about the item! Well, guess what – we never outgrow that urge to show off a special item. Residents love to bring a treasured item to show and tell the group about its history.

One woman at an assisted living community where I worked brought a sock monkey to show. She said her mother had made it in the early 1900s. It had survived many moves and had qualified as a "treasured item" she wanted to bring with her when she moved to the community. For those of you who don't know what a sock monkey is, the early ones were made with a brand of socks called Original Rockford Red Heel® socks. They are thick gray socks that have white tops, red heels, and white toes. I think I have seen fabric kits in craft catalogs recently, but the original monkeys were made from a pair of the socks and given to the children for Christmas or birthdays. The red heels became the monkey's mouth, and the white tops and toes were split and reassembled to form the monkey's feet and hands. Other pieces of the sock were fashioned into ears and sewn onto the head. A tail was fashioned from leftover strips of the sock. The sewn sock was stuffed with cotton or another kind of soft filling. The eyes were embroidered, or sometimes buttons were used for eyes. The monkeys were a familiar toy of several generations ago. Some of the other residents had at one time owned one and were amazed that this resident had retained hers through all the years.

A gentleman brought a belt buckle his father had made for him, decorated with a polished piece of deer antler from one of his father's hunting trips. Having a show and tell session can give a group information about each other and form bonds. How easy is it to forget a belt buckle decorated with a piece of deer antler – or the person to whom it belongs? Life is better when people learn about each other and begin to be interested in others' lives.

Storytelling

This fun group activity can create lots of laughter. The leader starts by saying, "Once upon a time..." The next person fills in the sentence, perhaps saying, "...there was a little girl." Then the next one adds something to the story, and around and around the story goes in the circle until someone provides a satisfactory ending. One such group produced a story about a man and a camel that lived in a swamp. Someone added some detail about quicksand, so the next person told how the man helped the camel out of the quicksand. This can even be done with two individuals, and it encourages creativity and fun.

If you lead a group and are fortunate enough to have access to a professional storyteller, the storyteller can tell a short story to demonstrate, then lead the group in telling some of their own. Storytelling is becoming a performing art in some areas, and there is even a website for the National Storytelling Network, where you can search for a professional in your area.

Reading

Reading to another person can be enjoyable for both the reader and the listener. If there is a regular time for reading aloud, that time is usually eagerly anticipated, especially if the listener has a choice in what is read. Readings can be magazine or newspaper articles, chapters from a book, short stories, or poetry. Humorous pieces are fun to share, as well as more serious items.

An activity director in a retirement community reads the questions from the daily newspaper's advice column at the residents' morning coffee group. Before reading the solutions given in the column, she lets the residents offer suggestions for solutions, then compares them to the ones from the column.

Reading and even writing poetry can be stimulating, especially when writing in a prescribed form, such as haiku. Many examples of haiku are available in book form. Haiku is often about nature. Reading some examples to the individual or group can let them hear the rhythm of the words, then they can begin to think about putting words together creatively.

The simple haiku form of a five-syllable first line, a seven-syllable second line, and a five-syllable third line can be quickly learned, and when the leader of a group stands with a chalkboard or a flip chart to record suggestions for lines, or an individual caregiver writes as a person tries creating lines, some beautiful poems can be the result. An example is:

Crimson leaves sweep down
Layering grass with color.
Lightweight fall blanket.

One assisted living community used haiku reading and writing as a group activity for several months, and a multitude of lovely poems were written by the residents. One memorable moment during this activity was to watch the residents count the syllables on their fingers – five, seven, five – as a resident read a poem. If someone said too many syllables, the group members were quick to point that out.

One woman read her poem, including the five-syllable line – "Spring has gone to bed." Another resident, who was from the Deep South, said with a delightful drawl, "Well, that's not right, because 'bay-ud' has two syllables." After the laughter subsided, the compassionate and tactful leader led a brief discussion about regional speech patterns.

The poems the group creates over the months can be saved by the leader, then typed, copied, and bound into a small booklet to be distributed at the front desk as an example of the diverse creative activities offered and the creativity exhibited by residents. Family members would love this.

Laughing

Laughter brightens dispositions. Journalist Norman Cousins used laughter as an experiment in self-healing in 1979, when he was diagnosed with arthritis. His book, *Anatomy of an Illness*, described his experiment. While there was some controversy concerning his claims, some physicians have since promoted the effect of laughter as medicine as well. Research has supported many of their claims about the effects of laughter on people's physical health as well as mental health. It is difficult to remain depressed very long when laughing heartily.

Humor and laughter are gaining wide attention these days, resulting in movements such as Laughter Yoga International, a world-wide organization to promote laughter. There are laughter clubs, gatherings of people who sit around and laugh (check out their website at www.laughteryoga.org, if this sounds unbelievable). At first forcing laughter can seem odd, but as soon as one person begins laughing, the laughter becomes contagious, and soon a whole roomful of people can be laughing.

The short-term physical benefits of laughter, according to a group of doctors at Mayo Clinic, can be many, including stimulating your heart, lungs, and muscles and increasing calming endorphins, as well as stimulating circulation and aiding muscle relaxation. Longer-term physical benefits can include improving your immune system and helping relieve pain. Emotional benefits include helping one to connect with other people and lessening depression and anxiety.

Writing Life Stories

Okay, I have saved the best activity (maybe I should say the one closest to my heart) for last. I believe this to be one of the most satisfying things a person can do in the later years of life.

Erik Erikson, a psychologist who developed a theory of life development in the 1950s, said that at some time in middle to later adulthood (he called the stage "Maturity") we face a task he termed "generativity," meaning having the urge to expand our influence and contribute to future generations. This can actually be *creating* future generations, as in having and raising children, or it can be *teaching* future generations and encouraging them. Erikson said if an individual does not engage in generativity of some kind, the alternative is self-absorption, an unhealthy turning inward and focusing only on oneself. Writing life stories, telling about beliefs, values, and learning experiences is one form of giving something to future generations.

Erikson also said the later years of life (he called this stage "Old Age") involved the task of "ego integrity." When Erikson used the word "integrity," he was not referring to morality or a character quality, but his meaning came from the root word "integration," or a blending of the various events and experiences of life to make a satisfying portrayal of a person's life; in other words, "integrating" the pieces of one's life to make a satisfying whole. The alternative, Erikson says, is to develop despair, resulting in low life satisfaction in old age. If one can look back on his life and enjoy the successes while acknowledging some failures, he can see that his life has, overall, been a series of learning experiences that has made him who he is, and he can be satisfied with the outcome.

My doctoral dissertation dealt with this subject, and showed statistically that when people in later life write their life stories, their life satisfaction increases. I taught classes to elderly women in retirement and assisted living communities on how to write their life stories for their families. In this case the research involved women, but there is reason to believe the same or a similar result would occur with men. Men were invited, and some participated in the classes, but the number of men was not sufficient to make a statistical analysis.

Some participants wrote on a computer, and some wrote in longhand on notebook or tablet paper. They had a great deal of fun with this project and enjoyed reading brief portions aloud to the rest of the class. They also had a great deal of enjoyment when they were able to present their families with a written record of portions of their life. Family members did not care whether there were grammatical errors or punctuation errors – they were ecstatic to have these gifts. After all, wouldn't those of you reading this book love to have a written record of your grandparents' or great-grandparents' lives?

Some examples of ways to spark memories are: "What was your favorite toy? Why was it special?" "Tell about your most memorable birthday," "What character quality has helped you most in your life, and why?" "Do your spiritual or religious beliefs include a higher power? If so, do you believe it is important that people believe in one? Why or why not?" "What was the happiest time of your life, and why?" "Tell about your greatest disappointment. Then tell about an event that brought you great happiness," "Which is your favorite holiday? What special memories do you have of celebrating that holiday?" "What advice would you give to young people today?"

Many more questions can be asked of a person to help him write about the important aspects of his life and begin to put the pieces of his life together for future generations. Most descendants would be delighted to receive such a gift.

Author Lois Duncan tells another story, indicating some offspring are pleased, others maybe not so pleased: "Florence, an elderly member of our church, was diagnosed with terminal cancer. She confided to me that she'd kept diaries ever since her teens. I typed the contents, (it took me literally months to decipher the horrible handwriting and set her story on paper), ran off copies, and had them inexpensively bound. Those journals contained some startling revelations – in her youth, Florence had done some outrageous things.

"Our church then held a book signing at which Florence was honored and all 100 copies sold. But it didn't stop there. People who bought the book told others about it, and those people wanted copies, too. The demand became so great that we did a second printing and then a third one. Florence was written up in the paper and was starring at book signings all over town.

"Her adult children were horrified and tried to close down publication, but Florence told them to go to Hell. She was having the time of her life. In fact, she was having so much fun that she decided not to die. And she DIDN'T DIE! To the amazement of her doctors, the huge tumor in her belly began to shrink and eventually vanished. The last time I saw her she was 92 years old, standing on a ladder, hand-painting the outside of her house."

While this is an exceptional story (and Lois tells it well), and I can't (and don't) promise that writing people's life stories will help them overcome cancer or any disease or medical condition (note the disclaimer), I can say with certainty that one's life story is a gift that only that individual can create and give, and when encouraged, many can produce treasured memoirs for their families and gain great satisfaction from doing so. Any caregiver has the opportunity to encourage and/or help a patient (perhaps via family members?) write or record portions of her life. I can't help wishing I could have included Florence in my dissertation, as that would have shown without a shadow of a doubt that writing and distributing her story increased her life satisfaction.

Many of these activities can be modified to fit the needs of the individual and can be as beneficial and enjoyable for the caregiver as for the patient. Dive into the opportunity to interact with those for whom you are given the caregiving responsibility. Enthusiasm and fun and joy have been found to be contagious!

CHAPTER 8

Understanding and Caring for Patients with Alzheimer's Disease and Other Dementias

Dementia is an umbrella term that covers impaired or lost memory resulting from many conditions. That scourge, dementia, whether caused by Alzheimer's Disease, a vascular accident, an injury, or another brain problem, is a loss that is recognized when the mistakes become too numerous to ignore. They can be rationalized up to a point, then the patient or his family and friends begin to realize there is something drastically wrong with his thinking processes. At first it is explained by saying, "Oh, I forgot," or "Oh, silly me." All of us make mistakes and do forgetful things, so we laugh them off, calling them "senior moments" until they begin to interfere with our functioning.

Mild cognitive impairment (MCI) is diagnosed when tests show a decline in thinking processes that may be worrisome at times but which does not greatly impinge on a person's daily activities. MCI can be, but is not always, a precursor of Alzheimer's Disease. Tests are usually done to determine whether it is a condition that can be remedied, such as a nutrition or medication issue, or whether there is another explanation such as stress.

When these incidents become frequent and interfere with functioning, the one whose memory is deteriorating has a window of time in which she knows something is wrong, but can't quite figure out what it is. There is confusion, worry, and frustration at not being able to function as well as before. The loss is beginning to be realized but not yet understood. It can be several weeks to several months to several years, but for that length of time, while she is realizing something is wrong, the decline is mystifying to her – and sometimes terrifying.

With much energy and effort, she tries to keep up with people whose memories are still intact, trying to be "normal" and not allowing others to notice she is different. Notes and reminders are written and posted by the telephone, on the dresser mirror, and on scraps of paper lying around. She realizes the need to make notes, but sometimes forgets to look at them. She feels inferior, not quite able to keep up, although making a valiant effort. This is perhaps the cruelest time of dementia, before it has developed to the point of leaving its victim in a state of not knowing that she does not know. Often the spouse will try to hide or deny the change in his partner, covering for forgotten words or abilities, not wanting others to notice her forgetfulness.

My first husband, Paul, had leukemia, as I've said. He also became very forgetful. It bothered him, but it was only after a couple of events that he realized something was terribly wrong.

Once he started for our veterinarian's familiar office to pick up some medication for our cat. He was gone a long, long time, and I became worried. Finally he drove into our driveway. I asked, "Did you get it okay?" He was near tears and said, "I never could find the vet's office." He said he went up one street and down another and never did see the office. He had been there many times.

Another troublesome time was when he went to pick up a pair of his slacks at the dry cleaners. It, too, was a very familiar place to both of us. He drove out of the driveway, but was back in a very short time – too short a time to have gotten to the cleaners and back – and was without the slacks. I asked if he'd had car trouble, and again, near tears, he admitted he couldn't remember how to get to the cleaners.

After that, I was our driver. We scheduled a neurological examination soon after these events, with an MRI, to eliminate the presence of a tumor or brain lesion, which might be evidence that the cancer had metastisized. In the absence of indications of tumor or lesion problems, but with white tangles showing up on the MRI, the diagnosis was mild cognitive impairment, with the possibility of evolvement into Alzheimer's Disease. The neurologist prescribed a common medication for memory problems, and we had the prescription filled, but it upset Paul's stomach. His oncologist recommended we discontinue it under the circumstances, as Paul had the most aggressive form of leukemia and the physician felt the memory problem was the least of our worries. Besides, others with leukemia in the support group we attended had also reported memory lapses, and had begun to refer to those instances as "chemo brain," thought to be caused by some of the treatments. As time went on, it did indeed prove to be one of the least of our worries, but was in many ways very frightening to Paul.

Mary Galvez, a Certified Care Manager and National Certified Guardian, said one of her clients with early dementia put it this way, "Loss of identity causes imbalance to happen." She reports, "When he said this, it hit me in the solar plexus. So powerful!" She said another memorable statement made to her by a client describing his dementia experience was, "This is so f***ing weird." She says that's probably the best dementia description she's ever heard. (Personal communication, Mary Galvez, October 9, 2013)

At this point, for that window of time in which the loss is realized, dementia is one of the greatest losses experienced by a person – the loss of self. I can only imagine Paul's frustration and bewilderment and worry at not being able to find the once-familiar vet's office or the dry cleaners.

If someone living alone develops dementia, it may be a neighbor or friend who notices the changes. Family members often do not want to admit the developing of dementia until it can no longer be denied. Over a period of time when their mother forgets to pay her bills, forgets to take her medications, or forgets and leaves the stove on, it becomes necessary for the family to take action for mom's safety and welfare.

If a spouse develops dementia, for all practical purposes it throws the other spouse into experiencing many of the secondary losses discussed in Chapter 3, by virtue of being the only one who has the cognitive functioning level to handle the financial affairs and everyday life of the couple. Sometimes the caregiving is managed at home, but sometimes it becomes too much for the spouse to handle. When the family recognizes that situation, a conference with the functioning spouse may lead to either frequent respite care for the one with dementia at a daycare center for seniors, or full-time residency at a memory care community equipped and trained to care for people with dementia. This decision is almost always traumatic for the family, for a variety of reasons.

Perhaps you are one of those family members, usually one or more of the children, who have in the past promised you'd never move a parent or loved one out of her home and into a facility of any kind. If you have not already made a promise like this, I urge you never to make that promise. No one knows what the future holds, and in some cases, it may be the most logical, safe, and responsible alternative. I have dealt with clients in my practice suffering from intense guilt about breaking such a promise to a parent, even when there seemed to be no other choice to preserve the caregiver's health.

Even the prospect of developing dementia can be scary, especially for those who have a family member going through the process. Mary Martinez, a gerontologist and the owner of a caregiving agency, and whose mother suffers from dementia, emailed me: "Today some of the staff experienced the 'Virtual Dementia' tour (a simulated exercise in experiencing this dreadful disease first hand). I had been putting it off but ran out of excuses today. I was immersed in the world of dementia and given tasks to complete in a 10-minute period. The instructions were given only once, verbally.

"My tasks were to set a table for four, write a three sentence letter to family and put it in an envelope, find and fold white towels from a pile of laundry, find a white sweater in the closet and put it on, and pour half a glass of water and drink it. With limited vision, white noise in my ears, and gloved hands with 'arthritic' fingers along with pads in my shoes, I had to complete tasks in a dimly lit room. Ten minutes seemed like such a long time. It seemed to take so long to get everything done. I became anxious but kept repeating the instructions to myself, so scared I was going to screw up or forget something. I completed the tasks but came away with a much stronger understanding of what my mother is going through right now.

"During debriefing I was told no one ever completes all the tasks. I was asked why I thought I had completed them all. I cried when I realized it was fear. I don't want to be the next person in my family to get Alzheimer's. I was determined to get them done.

"I thought I was patient before...well, we all could learn to be even more patient. It was a real eye-opener, even for someone with so many years of experience. You never know until you walk in those shoes. I hope I never wear them for real!" (Personal communication, Mary Martinez, October 8, 2013)

Alzheimer's is the most expensive disease in the United States – not in drugs or other medical treatments, but in care. It is important to prepare for the expense by seeing that the patient's assets are assessed and protected. Practical matters have to be addressed, such as seeing an attorney and having a will and a durable power of attorney drawn. The durable power of attorney designates someone to act on the patient's behalf when he is no longer able to make financial decisions that are deemed wise. A separate power of attorney for health care purposes can be drawn, designating a different person, if desired, to make decisions regarding health care. If these decisions and documents are done while the patient is still considered able to make decisions, this can be a relatively simple process. If the patient has already reached the stage in which his decisions are questionable, the usual procedure is to have one, or sometimes two, physicians declare him incompetent to make his own decisions, and guardianship may then be given by the court to a qualified person, either a relative or a professional who manages guardianships. Most people would rather make those decisions for themselves while they are still able. (Many people make sure they have these documents in place well in advance of needing them, because accidents or serious illness can occur at any age and render those affected unable to make decisions or speak for themselves.)

When a person is developing dementia and realizes it, making sure these documents are in place can bring a sense of relief about the future, at least the practical aspect. Planning for the future is important, and knowing the people who will be handling one's affairs in the future can be comforting.

A woman had been diagnosed with mild cognitive impairment, which was progressing. She had been told she appeared to be headed toward Alzheimer's Disease, and she was coming to me for help in learning to deal with the terrible loss of self. When she first came to me, she asked what she should do. I asked her if she had made plans for her future (as described in the paragraphs above). She had not, and the future looked scary to her. I suggested she talk to her family about preparing documents providing for her financial and healthcare needs and designating the people she most trusted to make decisions when she was no longer able. To help her remember to speak to her family, I wrote notes on my pad and handed them to her, and made sure she gave them to her family member who had come to pick her up.

By the next visit, she had spoken with her family, they had taken care of those documents, and she was obviously relieved. She was still very sad about her condition, but she had provided for the things she would need. That alone gave her a great deal of comfort. She said, "Well, I may be losing myself, but at least I know now how things will be handled for me."

Dementia, especially Alzheimer's disease, is a unique condition in which the progression varies widely. Often there will be plateaus in which there is very little change, yet sometimes the sudden changes are dramatic.

At first there is forgetfulness, then gradually the patient loses the ability to function, even in the most basic daily activities such as eating, bathing, toileting, and speaking. The time for this progression can be months, but usually is measured by years, creating a long span of time in which the patient needs constant care.

Caring for a patient with Alzheimer's disease can be a real test of a caregiver's mettle. The same questions are asked many times a day, because the patient does not remember the answers, and does not even remember asking. Besides losing the memory of events and names, the patient eventually loses the memory of objects' usefulness, sometimes creating humorous situations, as in a book by Helen Hudson about her grandmother's dementia, when she was making unique table arrangements with the dishes, silverware, napkins, etc.

Sometimes, however, the memory loss can create troublesome situations. Loss of memory often causes the loss of inhibitions, because social protocol is forgotten. Examples are trying to eat inedible materials, not remembering the functions of a spoon or fork, using a cell phone to try to control the television, or forgetting how to use the bathroom. In one assisted living community I managed, a male resident mistook a large potted plant for a urinal and proceeded to "water" the plant. This is not unusual behavior in a dementia unit, and most caregivers in such situations are trained to expect the unexpected and gracefully take care of such a matter discreetly while trying to maintain the resident's dignity.

Memory loss can also cause a patient to lose his inhibitions regarding anger. Paranoia is common, with the patient blaming others for things she cannot find, accusing them of stealing items or hiding them.

My maternal aunt had Alzheimer's disease, and my mother was her caregiver. One night my aunt woke my mother and asked her where she had put my aunt's extra bedsheets. Mother had no idea what she was talking about. My aunt said, "I know you took my spare sheets and hid them from me, and I want you to get up and get them right now." Similar events went on for years, regarding items she accused my mother of either stealing or hiding.

The difficult thing for caregivers to realize and keep in mind is that this is the disease, not the patient, talking. It is very hard to keep from taking these kinds of accusations personally, especially when it is a family member and there are years of history between both people. My mother would call me, crying, after having had her feelings hurt by my aunt.

Finally the decision was made to arrange for my aunt to live in a nursing home, and that was traumatic for my mother. She felt she had failed as a caregiver, but of course, she hadn't. After some discussions about the characteristics of Alzheimer's disease and the commonalities of behaviors, Mother came to realize she had actually done a superb job for as long as she could. She came to see her situation with relief and began to get rested. Even though she visited her sister often in the nursing home, she was now able to pursue some of her own outside interests and finally get a good night's sleep.

In *Learning to Speak Alzheimer's*, by Joanne Koenig Coste, many suggestions and ideas for taking the changes in stride are given. Distracting the patient or agreeing with her is better than trying to argue, because when people have lost the ability to reason, arguing only escalates a situation. Agreeing with a patient with Alzheimer's disease, even when what he believes is not true, causes fewer issues than trying to convince him otherwise.

An example is when a patient says, "I had a nice visit with Mother this morning," but the caregiver knows the mother died years earlier. Rather than try to convince the patient her mother is dead, which would cause anxiety and possibly an argument, simply saying something like, "That must have been enjoyable," can be comforting to her. In *her* mind, she did have a visit with her mother.

Reality therapy, a method that used to be popular when I first began working in nursing homes and assisted living communities, consisted of trying to convince a patient who had lost the ability to reason that facts are facts. If the patient asked where someone was, and the person was a family member who had died, we were to try to convince her the person was dead. If the patient asked to go home, we were to try to convince him the nursing home was his home now. This almost always resulted in frustration for both the patient and the caregiver.

Naomi Feil, in her books on the subject of validation, details many ways to meet the patient in the world in which he now resides, validating his feelings and, in turn, diminishing his fears and frustrations. Trying to determine what *emotions* are being expressed by the patient helps the caregiver to choose the appropriate solution to many of the problem behaviors. Talking about sadness and offering a snack and beverage or combatting anger with a calming activity can be effective ways to handle questions or behavior.

This book cannot possibly go into all the techniques for managing memory loss patients, but some of the books I've mentioned in the References and Suggested Readings list can be very, very helpful. Experiment with suggested ways of making both yours and the patient's lives more comfortable.

Appropriate Activities

Activities for patients with Alzheimer's disease are as varied as the stages of the disease. What works for one may not work for another individual, and what works during one stage may not work for the next stage. Creativity and ingenuity on the part of the caregiver can be a valuable asset.

John Morley, M.D., director of geriatric medicine at St. Louis University, was instrumental in forming the Cardinals Reminiscence League, a group of baseball fans with early-stage Alzheimer's disease who gather to talk about baseball. It is thought to improve quality of life, outcomes, and perhaps even thought processes, Morley says. Reminiscence therapy is catching on nationwide, and the Alzheimer's Association is helping to expand such groups. Obviously this activity depends on the patient's ability to verbalize, or to enjoy hearing others speak.

In the home and even in some residential memory care communities that are designed with small kitchens, supervised food preparation activities can be managed by patients, depending on their abilities at the time. Taking the leaves off a head of lettuce and placing them on a plate; pinching the stems off fresh spinach or breaking green string beans into pieces preparatory to cooking – all these can help a patient feel valued, useful, and a contributor to the meal.

Gardening in raised beds designed for that purpose can be enjoyable for a patient with memory loss. Digging in the dirt provides a tactile experience, and being outdoors in good weather can be healthy. Care must be taken to choose plants that are not poisonous, as you can never be assured that the patient will not try to eat parts of the plant, especially if leaves or blooms are colorful and appear to be edible.

Using picture boards to tell a story may be used with even non-verbal patients, especially if the story is about something in which they were formerly interested or about which they were knowledgeable. Flannel boards on an easel are useful, with paper or felt figures that easily adhere to the flannel as the story is told.

One day I decided to take my song-leading talent (mentioned in Chapter 7) into the dementia side of the nursing home where I worked. Caregivers said it would never work, that the residents there did not even speak coherently, much less sing coherently, but I wanted to try. The first day I began to sing "You are My Sunshine," hoping some would want to follow along. Some began to move their mouths, but little sound came out.

The caregivers were watching with anticipation. One began to cover her mouth in surprise and point to one man. He had not said a word in years, suffering from Korsakoff's Syndrome, a form of dementia. To the surprise of all of us, he had begun to form the words and a faint melody was coming from his lips. Somewhere in the depths of his memory was this familiar song. Music can be a vehicle for reaching those buried, yet cherished, memories.

Depending on the patients' remaining abilities, some enjoy sorting things – buttons (although care must be taken to supervise, lest they try to put some in their mouths and swallow them), playing cards, blocks of various colors, or pictures cut out of magazines of various foods or clothing. Those who had clerical jobs may enjoy sorting and filing papers in file folders. Some may tire of this easily, but some, surprisingly, can enjoy engaging in this sorting activity for as much as an hour.

If a patient had been an accountant or another occupation having to do with numbers, giving him a calculator and a sheet of numbers to add may provide him with an interesting activity, again depending on his ability. If frustration begins to set in, another activity needs to be on hand for distraction, or perhaps it is snack time with a beverage.

Tactile sensations are important ways of keeping people in touch with parts of the environment that may have become foreign to them. Folding warm washcloths or napkins fresh out of the dryer may be comforting (and even helpful to the staff or family), or just stroking smooth velvet cloths or pillows.

One family made a "tactile board" of thin, lightweight plywood and rounded and smoothed the corners, to avoid skin tears. They divided it into quarters visually by gluing various items onto it, each about six inches square and each of a different color – one of purple velvet cloth, one of yellow terrycloth, one of blue satin cloth, and one of very fine sandpaper. It was interesting to see the patient carefully stroke each one, and even talk to the different squares – "nice" or "rough" or "baby" – whatever came to mind with regard to the different textures and colors.

If the patient enjoys television, funny movies or television sitcoms can encourage laughter, and that is good for anyone. Many patients love to watch their favorite sports/teams on TV, too, many times as a group with snacks and beverages. Sitting and watching with the patient provides companionship and entertainment and a time of mini-respite for the caregiver.

Eating Suggestions

Finger foods are good for snack time – pieces of fresh fruit, soft vegetables, cookies, cheese and crackers, or soft meat rolled up in bread or a tortilla – these enable them to bypass the frustration of dealing with silverware. Presenting one entreé at a time and serving small portions will simplify mealtime for dementia patients. Warm beverages need to be warm, not hot, as often the ability to determine how hot a beverage is can become foreign to the patient, and he can burn his lips or tongue.

If chewing appears to cause pain and the patient is past the stage in which she can verbalize that pain, caregivers need to be observant and see that she has an examination of the mouth and gums, to be sure there is not a problem with ill-fitting dentures or a sore inside the mouth. Usually a facial expression will alert the caregiver to evidence of discomfort.

Bathing Suggestions

Most patients with dementia become fearful of bathing. They forget the process, and the sound of rushing water in either the shower or a tub seems menacing to them. When they first begin to need help bathing, they may still be cognitively functional enough to feel embarrassed that someone has to see them naked, and that may be a part of their aversion to bathing.

Sometimes taking time to distract them before bath time can be helpful, even telling them a story as you walk them to the tub or shower. Having the tub already filled to a comfortable level with warm water can save time and eliminate the fear of hearing the water filling the tub. Be sure to have the towels and clothing already at hand, because any delay can cause the patient to become frustrated and anxious.

Entering a shower can be frightening to someone with dementia. Soothing music on a CD player in the bathroom (if using a plug-in type, place it well away from any water, for safety's sake) may be a help in calming her. Be careful in a shower to rinse the soap off quickly, as it can make a body slippery and difficult to hold onto in case of a fall.

Sleeping Suggestions

Sleeping can become troublesome as the disease progresses. A condition known as "sundowning" may occur, causing the patient to be up and about while other people are sleeping. Keeping a dim light on in the house or in the hallway or common areas can help prevent falls. Keeping the outside doors secure with locks that are placed out of reach or are operated with a keypad can ensure the patient does not go outdoors.

I've said my mother was the caregiver for her sister, who had Alzheimer's disease. For the first couple of years my aunt lived in her own home, and my mother lived nearby in her own home, going over to care for my aunt only during the day. This schedule came to an end when neighbors noticed my aunt out one night in only her nightgown, wandering around the neighborhood. From that time on, my mother had to stay with her sister all the time, and several kinds of latches were installed on the front and back doors, so that my aunt could not figure out the sequence and open the doors.

There are techniques for coping with sundowning, such as taking the patient for a walk before bedtime to create enough fatigue to enable her to sleep soundly, but sundowning is a pretty universal stage and needs to be anticipated. Some preventive measures can be implemented, such as placing anything that can be harmful out of sight and preferably out of reach or in a locked cabinet. Motion sensors that alert a sleeping caregiver that the patient is up can be helpful. Sometimes a soothing handrub with lotion or soft music will induce him to get back into bed and go back to sleep.

Respite Suggestions

It was uplifting to get a letter from Norman Lindholm, a pastor friend in Ohio. He and his two daughters investigated some daytime respite care for Norm's wife, Lou, who has Alzheimer's disease (personal communication, Norman Lindholm, January 10, 2014). They went together and interviewed the owner/director, Marsha Shepherd, of a memory care community in their vicinity that offers respite care. Norm said, "Marsha's reputation, plus our assessment of our interview to consider enrolling Lou, helped us decide it was worth a try – just for maintenance care." They report it worked out so much better than they had expected.

Norm said, "Interestingly, being with 24+ other 'limited' people evidently created a non-threatening environment. As it developed, it is appealing to Lou to join them. The owner/leader and all her staff are pro-active at interacting with and engaging all clients. That's their philosophy, to activate clients while providing hygiene and care. This was totally unexpected for us. For Lou, there's no other cognitive improvement, but she is amazingly much more interactive now. It is certainly better for her [and us] at least for now."

Norm issues a caution, however, and says, "We consider Marsha, her program, and her staff so unique we are not confident many other adult daycare centers would yield such benefits. We just don't know, and don't know the field. I'm sure we cannot write a 'blank check' saying daycare is everyone's happy solution. My estimate is that Marsha Shepherd and her Alternative Care Center staff are probably above average for quality positive benefits. We saw Lou's comfort there become evident after a couple of months, and her interactivity improved by three months. A dedicated process was involved. The 'wow' benefit is a tribute to the whole staff initiating their outstretched friendly acceptance – and ACC's activity agenda engaging each client and the group – with morning welcome, buoyant physical stretches/motions, a creative projects/activities room (simple crafts), lunchtime, rest period, games, transportation, and more. I'm convinced ACC is unique, not the average. While ACC provides quality care for Lou and provides my daughters and me with respite time, perpetual home care for Lou is still necessary."

I agree with Norm that while respite daycare of that quality may be difficult to find and might not work as well for some families, it is worth talking with the directors of such communities to assess how day care might benefit not only the patient, but the family as well. Apparently it has made a difference in Lou's enjoyment of life and given Norm and his daughters some well-needed respite from constant caregiving duties. Your local Alzheimer's Association chapter may be able to provide you with the names of some centers in your area that offer short or long-term respite care so that you can make an appointment to gather information about their program.

This chapter has hit only the high points of dementia and caring for someone with memory loss, but there are many good books focusing entirely on that specific topic, some of which are listed in the References and Suggested Readings list at the back of this book. Let me reiterate that Alzheimer's and related diseases or conditions causing memory impairment can last many, many years. Unless another disease intervenes and causes death, eventually Alzheimer's disease will continue to progress until the patient is bedfast and unable to eat or drink. I will touch on this end stage in Chapter 10, which discusses the dying process.

CHAPTER 9

Coping with the Stress of Caregiving

CAREGIVING IS A TOUGH JOB, even when you love the person you are serving. Stress and fatigue are only two of the common symptoms caregivers face. It is important to balance your life as much as possible in order to do a good caregiving job. We will look at some of the effects of caregiving and some practical ways to take care of yourself while you are taking care of someone else.

LOSSES FOR THE PATIENT

The patient is suffering losses, as I have described in earlier chapters. It may be primarily a loss of health, either sudden or gradual. It almost surely results in diminished independence, which often causes irritability and anger in the patient. These situations serve as a backdrop and set the stage for stress for both the patient and the one who is responsible for her care.

LOSSES FOR CAREGIVERS

Caregivers face losses, too, with either the eventual death of the patient, or in the case of dementia, the loss of the personality of the person they once knew. Clients come into my office grieving someone with whom they had developed a close relationship through their daily/nightly time spent with them. Some clients have to take time off from their jobs to learn to cope with losing a series of patients assigned to them through an agency. It is not often that people recognize the grief caregivers experience, even if the patient is not a member of the family. There is a delicate balance between professional caregiving and the human side of us all. We think of it as a profession or, in the case of caring for a family member, as a service of obligation or love, but many hours spent with someone performing the basic needs of life almost surely results in the grief response when the patient is no longer either cognitively functional or alive. Besides the adjustments faced in these events, many other situations in the personal life of a caregiver can come about during the course of the caregiving duties, causing great stress.

Caregiving is physically demanding and can cause injuries from lifting and bending. Your physical health is important. Care for it by eating well, resting and sleeping well, and getting some aerobic exercise such as walking.

Occasionally we see caregivers whose relationship with the client becomes emotionally entangled with a mixture of affection and uncomfortable intimacy. Those of us who have children know this entanglement – we love and care for our children, yet we are responsible for helping them with the most intimate functions such as changing diapers or toileting and bathing. We take that in our stride, as do they, because they are children and will outgrow the need.

When performing these functions for adults however, there is usually some discomfort on the part of both caregiver and patient. We know it is necessary and they require help, but it strips away the last vestige of independence and privacy of a person, and often creates a dilemma of how to balance the adult communication and dignity with the help for these everyday needs. Talented is the caregiver who can carry this off successfully, and sometimes even for those persons who can do so, it takes an unrecognized emotional toll.

The freedom of the caregiver, particularly a family caregiver, is compromised. Sometimes a rigid routine of care competes with a need to get other household tasks accomplished. Caregiving can also be isolating, with little chance for outside connections with others.

There is the challenge faced by family caregivers who need to be employed but who can't afford to hire someone to help with the caregiving. Sixty-one percent of caregivers over the age of 50 also work outside the home.

Amy Goyer cared for her mother, who had had a stroke, until her mother's recent death, and her father, who has Alzheimer's disease, while holding down a job as a writer and consultant. She suggests that employed family caregivers talk to their employers and explain the situation. Perhaps the work hours can be flexible, or perhaps part-time hours or job-sharing can be arranged. Telecommuting is an option for some occupations. The Family Medical and Leave Act through the Department of Labor is available under certain circumstances, and may or may not provide some paid time off. There may be provisions in some states for family caregivers to be paid for caregiving. For further information on combining family caregiving and employment, see Boyer's book, *Juggling Work and Caregiving*, available as a free eBook at the time of this writing, at AARP.org/CaregivingBook.

Finances can be stressful for many people even under the best of conditions, but when caregiving is combined with a limited income and escalating bills and debt, balancing a budget and continuing to function can become overwhelming. Sometimes the stress level affects the quality of care.

Caring for a family member with whom you had dreams for future activities and companionship means the loss of many of those dreams. One wife had dreamed of going to Ireland to check into some genealogy findings, but when her husband became terminally ill, she knew that trip, as well as others with him, would never take place, adding a sadness and sense of additional loss to her caregiving duties.

For caregivers with young children, caring for elderly parents or other relatives can become a complex matter of priorities. How do you manage the shuttling to school and various activities when

Grandmother can't be left alone? Or what about a school play that is scheduled at the time of a doctor's appointment? Many other scenarios may complicate trying to juggle caring for two different generations, and this juggling creates stress.

Grief and Depression

At other points in this book I have outlined the symptoms associated with grief: Sadness and crying, anger and irritability, sleep disturbances, losing or gaining weight, vague and transient aches and pains, lack of concentration, loss of interest in things formerly enjoyed, and fatigue and low energy, to name a few. Depression, while it can be a component of grief, can occur for different reasons, often triggered by stress.

There is situational depression, which is temporary, exhibiting the same or similar symptoms as grief. Caregiving can evolve into depression if not given attention.

There is also clinical depression, which can exhibit the same or similar symptoms of grief and situational depression, plus most of the following symptoms nearly every day for at least two weeks: Feelings of worthlessness, excessive or unreal guilt, feelings of hopelessness, and thoughts of suicide. Caregivers who have grieved many losses and experienced constant stress for a long period of time sometimes exhibit clinical depression.

Stress Management Skills

There are things you can do that will mitigate your stress. First we'll look at skills to relieve the temporary type of depression, then additional helps for clinical depression.

Situational Depression (temporary)

Reduce Your Responsibilities if You Can

Some things we think have to be done can wait or do not need to be done at all. I was a young housewife and mother in the era before permanent pressed fabrics for clothing became available. As a result, I had a big stack of ironing to do every Tuesday (my self-imposed schedule – you know, wash on Monday, iron on Tuesday, clean house on Wednesday – that era – okay, so most of you reading this do not even know what I'm talking about – life was very different back then). Even when clothing that didn't have to be pressed came on the scene, I kept ironing the old things. Then it dawned on me that gradually I could replace items of clothing for the whole family with things that didn't need to be ironed at all. That saved almost a day every week that could be used doing other things. This, of course, is only an example. But really, much we do is not as essential as we have come to believe.

When time and stress levels are of the essence, try to prioritize and do only the really "we cannot live if these things are not done" chores. Paper plates are a great time saver for family caregivers (note to family and friends – they also make a nice gift!). Keeping the house reasonably picked up and clean, rather than spotless, is okay. It is not a sign of weakness or failure to ask for help. You can copy this paragraph and put it on the fridge to remind you!

Practice Mindfulness

I have mentioned mindfulness in other chapters, but it is a wonderful stress reliever. Focus on your normal breathing (requires no equipment except what you already possess) while silently thinking, "Breathing serenity in, breathing anxiety out, breathing serenity in, breathing anxiety out,..." Closing your eyes helps keep out distractions. If thoughts such as "I need to be doing the wash" or "I must keep that appointment tomorrow" or "I forgot to put something on the grocery list" begin to come to mind (as they will), just notice them, acknowledge them, then let them go and go back to focusing on your breathing.

Everyone will have these intruding thoughts, because our minds are working all the time, so if you have them, you are not failing in the exercise. Your breathing time is a time of "being," not "doing." You do not attempt to accomplish anything associated with your thoughts, just notice they are there and continue to focus on your breathing. You can set a kitchen timer for five minutes. Studies have shown that doing this exercise just five minutes twice a day over eight weeks can actually build new neural pathways in your brain and cause a portion of the brain, the insula, to become more active, as evidenced by brain imaging. The insula is the part of the brain that, among other functions, helps us be empathetic, helping us connect to others.

This exercise also calms you and helps you see things from a different perspective. I caution you to breathe normally, not faster than normal, lest you hyperventilate. Five minutes will at first seem like an eternity, but the more you do this, the more you will begin to look forward to your mindfulness time. Almost anyone, even someone with myriad caregiving duties, can carve out ten minutes in a day if she determines to do so.

I have clients who say mindfulness has revitalized them while calming and relaxing them and has changed the way they look at life. There are many mindfulness exercises, but this is a basic and very easy one to practice daily.

Exercise Appropriately

I know caregiving requires many steps a day, but the kind of exercise I mention here is something as simple as taking a walk around the block, or even around the outside of the house. This kind of steady, continuous exercise causes your body to produce endorphins that are calming chemicals. They are known to produce feelings of well-being. Walking on a treadmill will enable you to be available to the patient you are with and create valuable endorphins at the same time. However, one study showed that walking outside in nature and noticing things like the grass, trees, birds, and clouds is more beneficial than walking indoors on a machine, in a mall, or in downtown city areas. Nature seems to be a healing agent.

Reach Out to Others

Having a good friend or relative who will allow you to talk and vent a bit on the phone or during a visit is a help for stress. There is one caution here – listening to your venting can get tiresome for friends or relatives, so try to keep your conversations short. You don't want them to dread hearing from you.

Ask for Help

Even the most self-sufficient person needs help once in a while, so don't try to be Superman or Superwoman and do absolutely everything yourself. If you feel you are stressed about meals, ask friends if they are willing to make a double recipe once in a while and bring you dinner. Most people are delighted to help occasionally, and it can be a real service to you when you are overtired at the end of a day.

When I was caring for my mother toward the end of her life, she could not be left alone. I occasionally asked a friend to come and sit with her for half an hour while another friend and I went to a drive-in restaurant for a milkshake. Just that little bit of time was helpful to me, and my friends were glad to help in that way.

You might need someone to come and stay for an hour or two during the day to allow you to get a haircut, go to the grocery store, exercise, go to a movie, or go into another room to read for a while. People won't realize how important these times can be for you unless you verbalize your need or unless they have also been a caregiver. Some people are kind enough to offer, and if so, take advantage of this blessing.

Be Patient with Yourself

This goes back to the "not everything has to be done" paragraphs above. If you can't get everything done, realize not everything has to be done, and you are only human.

Laugh When You Can

This was brought out in the chapter on activities for seniors, but it applies to caregivers as well. Laughter is good for you – even a smile on your face is good for you. Remember studies show that even faking a smile can make you feel happier.

Watch funny movies with the patient – it will also benefit her. Laugh at yourself when you do something wrong – lighten your burden with laughter.

Arrange for Respite Care

This has also been brought out in an earlier chapter, but many retirement communities or agencies can accommodate people for just a day or a few hours. As mentioned in Chapter 8, Lou Lindholm's family has been fortunate to find an appropriate place that can provide benefits to Lou while also giving the family some time off from caregiving.

Janice Wood reported on a study at Penn State in which Steven Zarit, Ph.D., professor and head of human development and family studies, found that using adult day services seems to give caregivers a break that can reduce their chronic stress. Adult day services programs may be provided by senior communities, where seniors who need supervision may stay for part of the day, have snacks and lunch, and participate in appropriate planned activities with other seniors.

Caring for a patient with dementia can be extremely stressful, and the use of adult day services seems to have an effect of lowering anger and reducing depression in family caregivers on the days they take a break and use the services. Some senior communities will provide respite care for a weekend or even a week while you take a mini-vacation. Some respite from your duties will refresh you and make you a better and happier caregiver.

Journal Your Feelings

Writing your feelings has been shown to relieve stress. Simply the act of getting them down on paper, in black and white, so that you can see them, relieves stress. We don't know exactly why journaling helps, but we know that it does. It does not have to be done in a beautiful, bound book. A spiral notebook or tablet does the job just as well. Write as much or as little as you want.

Once during a stressful time in my life, I journaled in a yellow spiral notebook. I remember one entry ended with my scratching my pen across the paper and tearing it, not intentionally, but I was getting my feelings of frustration out in a physical way. At some point I decided to destroy that notebook to spare my family the sadness of someday finding it and seeing how stressed I had become. But at the time, journaling was a life-saver to me. It can be an important outlet for caregivers.

Join a Support Group

There are support groups for almost any kind of need. It is often difficult for a caregiver to get to a support group, but if you want to try it, perhaps a friend or relative would come and stay with your patient while you attend a meeting. Groups are not for everyone, but some people are helped in that way. Many retirement communities, churches, and various non-profits sponsor support groups. Calling around or searching the internet may help you find one you'd like to try.

Do Something Creative

This is one of the most delightful remedies for stress. If you do embroidery or other kinds of handwork, if you paint, or if you have some kind of craft that you enjoy, I encourage you to engage in it periodically. There is value in creating, and it is therapeutic. I often have my clients write poetry, and some are quite talented. Whatever you do that is creative and that you enjoy – quilting, scrapbooking; working jigsaw, crossword, or Sudoku puzzles; writing parts of your memoir; or [you fill in this blank with what especially appeals to you] – will relieve stress.

When my first husband was having a series of treatments, I spent untold hours in waiting rooms. I bought little kits of crewel embroidery, just small projects at a time that were either small pillows or pieces that could be framed. Over a period of a few months, I completed many of them and gave them as gifts. It kept my hands busy and was a constructive therapeutic activity.

When he was hospitalized in later months, I kept Sudoku, crossword, and word-finder puzzle books, as well as a novel, in the bag I carried with me every day. While he slept, I engaged my brain in solving puzzles or reading.

We have a built-in mechanism for dealing with stress. Creative endeavors engage the right sides of our brains – focusing on satisfaction, beauty, esthetics, and harmony.

Clinical Depression (ongoing, chronic)

All the suggestions above are helpful for clinical depression caused by caregiving, with some essential additions. It is necessary that you have a thorough physical exam to rule out any physical health issues. It is also necessary that if your physician prescribes medication, such as antidepressants, you take them exactly as prescribed. Counseling by a licensed professional may provide some tools for coping and help you see things from a different perspective.

Caregiving is a demanding, stressful, sometimes seemingly unending task that may not seem appreciated by the patient. If you are a caregiver employed by an agency or senior community, if you are an independent caregiver, or if you are a family member caring for a loved one, rest assured that your services are one of the finest contributions you can make to humanity.

CHAPTER 10

Looking Toward the End

NEEDLESS TO SAY, THE END result for each of us is death. We may not like to think about it or talk about it or read about it, but the fact is that each of us will die, including the patient or patients for whom you are a caregiver. It is very difficult for most people to contemplate their own death, even when they care for someone who is dying. It is what happens to other people.

In this day of medical science and technology we expect that someone will be able to prevent death. We have talked about how anger is a part of grief, and almost any physician or nurse can testify that some families harbor anger toward them because a loved one has died. Doctors and nurses are trained to delay death, but no one has the power to prevent death indefinitely.

This chapter is not about delaying death or even trying to prevent it, but will address the issue of dying itself and the attitudes of dying people toward death. Probably the most read, taught, and discussed speaker and writer on death and how people approach it is Elizabeth Kübler-Ross. After being with many, many dying people over many years, Kübler-Ross developed a theory of stages that dying people go through.

Her theory of dying as experienced by a dying person is composed of five stages – denial, anger, bargaining, depression, and acceptance. I'll discuss these stages briefly, although most people know them and can recite them.

Denial – In Kübler-Ross' initial stage, there is shock and disbelief. The diagnosis does not seem real and may be discounted. Some persons seek several physicians' opinions, feeling a mistake has been made.

Anger – Her second stage consists of anger – toward God or medical science or perhaps toward the person himself, for not taking better care of himself. The anger can extend to whomever and whatever is at hand.

Bargaining – Kübler-Ross says many dying people try to bargain with God or whatever higher power to which they ascribe. "I'll be a better person, if only you'll let me live…" "I'll atone for all my misdeeds, if only…"

Depression – When the reality of the situation begins to descend on the patient, she may fall into depression, dwelling on the magnitude of losing her life, and therefore losing everything.

Acceptance – At some point, Kübler-Ross says, most people come to terms with the diagnosis and the inevitability of death.

(While this theory seems to hold reasonably well for most dying people, it has been extrapolated by some therapists and theorists to apply to *grieving* people, which is not the way Kübler-Ross intended it at all. Some parts of her theory may apply to grieving the loss of someone close to you, but what about her third stage, "bargaining?" What is a grieving person bargaining for? The return of the loved one? We easily see the folly of that, yet Kübler-Ross's theory is continually mis-applied to grievers.)

Not every dying person goes through all these stages. While many will go through the stage of denying and doubting the original diagnosis, some will not feel a great deal of anger, or experience a bargaining stage. The depression stage is fairly predictable, as the person contemplates losing everything, absolutely *everything*, they have ever known. The peace of acceptance brings a calm that some observers interpret as failure to realize the situation. I prefer to see it as the time when a person has made peace with the reality of death and has taken care of the things that are important to him.

When a patient comes to accept the reality that he has reached the point in the illness when death is inevitable, he realizes he is no longer in control. Some people compensate for this helpless feeling by trying to control other people or events. They may become demanding, or become angry when care is not provided in the way they expect.

Some exert this control constructively by wanting to write, or help write, their obituary or make final arrangements. Some go into great detail, planning their own funeral or memorial service. They may have made their wishes known about either burial or cremation. If burial, they may have chosen the place; if cremation, they may have a special place they want their cremains buried or scattered (cremains is the technical word for what remains after cremation, although the term ashes is often used – cremains is more accurate, as besides some ash, there will also be tiny bone fragments in the residue), or they may express a wish to have them kept in someone's possession and neither buried nor scattered.

My first husband, Paul, had extended periods of hospitalization in which he had a lot of time to think. Each time he was hospitalized, we knew the end was drawing nearer. In his career he was an organized, detail-oriented manager, in control of people and events, and his behavior toward the end of his life was much the same. He knew, of course, that he could not prevent his death, but there were many things he could still control. I would say without question he had reached the acceptance stage, and he wanted to be fully involved in planning the end of his life.

During one hospitalization, he wrote his own obituary on a tablet. I went home and typed it and printed it for him to see. He edited it, and I retyped it. He listed the pallbearers and had me contact them to be sure they'd be willing to serve. All that was left out was the actual date of death. He had me ask the funeral director, who was also our friend, to come to his hospital room and bring pictures of caskets, so he could select the one he wanted. Then he asked me to go to the mortuary and look at the casket and make sure it was like the picture.

He designed his own memorial folder to be given out to people who attended his service. He selected the Bible verses he wanted inside the folder. He wanted a photo of the Sandia Mountains on the front. I took some photos, but they weren't the best, so I went to the phone book and found a professional photographer. He had a photo, and said he would bring it to the hospital for Paul to see. He arrived with the photo, a spectacular one, and Paul said that is what he wanted. I was prepared to pay the photographer for the use of the photo, but he would not take my check. He said his wife had died a few months earlier, and he wanted this photo to be his gift to Paul.

Paul had me ask the pastor who was to officiate at his service to come to the hospital room to confer about the service. He did. Later, after Paul had been discharged from the hospital and was on hospice care, he asked me to call our friend from the mortuary and the pastor and ask them to come to our home to plan the service, to make sure they knew what he wanted. Before they arrived, Paul had asked me to list the order of the service he wanted, and the approximate time each piece of the service would take, so he could see how long it would be and could make changes if he needed to.

Remember I said he was organized and detail-oriented? He had this list down to the minutes for each piece – soloist, sermon, a selection from a CD he loved, and finally a DVD he had made earlier in which he gave a brief account of his life. When our friend from the funeral home and the pastor arrived, I read them the order of the service, and they said they would do everything in their power to make it happen just the way Paul wanted it. Paul was pleased and at peace. He had controlled, as much as he could, what would happen even after his death. Now that he had planned everything, he seemed to relax. While this preparation may sound extreme to some people, it gave Paul the feeling of control he felt he was losing.

A few weeks later, when the time came for Paul's service, it happened just the way he had planned it. It was beautiful, and there were no glitches at all. After the service when I was standing in the foyer of the funeral home, our funeral director friend said, "Well, do you think Paul would have been pleased?" I said, "Yes, it went perfectly. Thank you." With a smile, he said, "Well, I don't think I could face Paul in Heaven if anything had gone wrong."

I see death notices and obituaries in the newspaper saying, "At her (or his) request, no service will be held." I always feel sad about that, because while the dying person may be trying to save his family the experience of a funeral, cut down on expense, or save their having to plan a service, he may be depriving them of a meaningful "good-bye" opportunity. Survivors need some kind of closing ceremony to mark the end of a lifetime. Even a simple get-together with friends and relatives can serve the purpose, but with no service of any kind, survivors are left without a marker for the finality of death.

When Kübler-Ross' theory is applied to dying people, many do experience some of the stages, but not necessarily in the order in which they are listed. They may go back and forth between stages, lingering longer within some, possibly bypassing some altogether. Some theorists now have added a sixth stage, to which they refer as a psycho-spiritual stage, that of transcendence. They purport a time near death in which dying people experience a serene peacefulness, and even visions, which seem to enable them to approach death with serenity and sometimes even eagerness.

My mother appeared to experience a vision a day or two before she died. She had been fairly unresponsive, but on an occasion when my daughter, my husband, and I were sitting at her bedside, she suddenly opened her eyes, raised her arms up toward the ceiling, and said, with a smile, "Oh look, they're showing me a little angel." Those were among her last words before she lapsed into a coma and died soon afterward. How can we doubt the "realness" of these kinds of experiences?

We are entering an era in which talking and thinking about the dying process is becoming more acceptable. There are groups that get together to discuss their thoughts and feelings about dying. There are workshops on dying. People seem to be wanting to come to grips with their feelings and fears about their own deaths. Death is a natural part of life and can be approached in that way. Gatherings called Death Cafes are being organized in some places, giving people an opportunity to gather for a meal and discuss death.

Speaking of fears about death, an interesting sidelight is that years ago there was such a fear of being buried alive that contraptions were invented to assure persons that if they revived, they would be able to communicate and be freed from the casket. One such invention by Russian Count Karnice-Karnicki in 1896, consisted of a tube that was inserted into the lid of the coffin and was attached to a mechanism in which the slightest movement of the chest set into motion a flag, light, and loud bell above ground to attract the attention of onlookers. Whether any were saved from the fate of being buried alive by this device is not recorded, at least not that I could find.

As I said, everyone will die. Whether we die quickly or linger for a time, the end result is the same. Different diseases and/or conditions dictate the general way in which death will come. Sometimes death is sudden, as in a heart attack or stroke. Generally, in the case of disease, the death is gradual – incapacitating, then ending in some time of being comatose. Other people never experience the comatose stage and continue to be alert and talkative up until they breathe their last breath. Victims of Alzheimer's disease, unless some other condition causes death, gradually decline in abilities until they are bedfast and are not able to eat or drink, because they can no longer swallow.

Some people in poor health and nearing death choose, whether voluntarily or involuntarily, to no longer eat or drink. If food is brought to them, they may refuse it. This decision often dismays family members, and they may insist on forcing the patient to eat, or insist that healthcare providers insert a feeding tube, or at least insist that intravenous fluids be administered.

The patient usually knows best when his body is at the stage of shutting down. Dying from starvation is not painful when the body no longer needs food or drink. When people can no longer eat, or no longer want to, feeding through a tube or an IV can make the last days very uncomfortable for them, because the body is losing its capacity to process food or liquid. The digestive system cannot handle food, because it is beginning the dying process. Often the additional fluid simply puts too great a demand on the diminishing function of the kidneys, resulting in bloating and discomfort for the patient. Toward the end there may not be a lot of urine or fecal matter produced, because the organs have ceased to function efficiently.

Restlessness, tossing, turning, picking at the bedclothes, and even trying to get out of bed may occur, because the brain may not be getting enough oxygen and the normal processes are disrupted. Agitation may be unsettling to the family or caregiver. My mother had periods like this while dying, and it calmed her for me to lie beside her in her double bed and lay my arm across her on top of the covers. My presence seemed to be comforting to her. My first husband also had periods of restlessness in which I would sit on the side of his bed and lay my arm across his legs on top of the covers. Just the light pressure indicating my presence seemed to be calming.

A caregiver can be aware of when the time has come for the patient's active dying and be respectful of the patient's desire not to eat or drink. Comfort measures are still taken, like moistening the lips from time to time, turning the patient in the bed to prevent pressure sores, and being sure moist or soiled pads or diapers are changed frequently. Soft music may be played, and voices can be kept soft, because often the hearing lingers even when the patient is comatose. Sometimes holding the patient's hand can be comforting. One of my friends once said, "When you hear I am dying, please come and hold my hand." I hope I hear about her impending death should she predecease me, and I will be there.

The breaths of a dying person will usually become less frequent and at times stop for a few seconds, ten to 20 or up to 40 seconds, then start again. A few seconds does not sound like a long time, but when you are attending dying patients, it can seem an eternity, and at times you will think they have died. This cycle of breathing is called Cheyne-Stokes pattern, and often there is a breathing "rattle" that occurs, caused by accumulated mucous that the body is unable to expel. Finally, the breathing does not resume, and the patient has died.

My mother displayed this breathing pattern as I sat at her bedside one day. I would hear her breathing, then nothing. I would look at her and become anxious, thinking, "Please start breathing," and another breath would come. However, about mid-afternoon, the space between breaths became longer and longer, and as I waited for her to catch her breath, I waited and waited and waited...and another breath never came.

If the patient is on hospice care, a hospice nurse is to be called when that last breath has been taken. The nurse will be the one to declare that death has occurred. If death occurs in a hospital, a qualified attendant at the hospital will certify death.

If the patient dies at home and isn't on hospice care, 911 has to be called, and the police and emergency medical technicians will visit the site before the body is allowed to be removed by the mortuary. This procedure is required in most, if not all, states.

At this writing, five states (Montana, New Mexico, Oregon, Vermont, and Washington) allow physician-assisted death, following certain protocols and ensuring that all guidelines have been followed. This book will not deal further with that topic, other than to make readers aware that some states allow choices in legally arranging one's own death.

While all of this discussion about dying may seem morbid, the actual attitudes of elderly about dying and death paint a more hopeful picture. In a study by Cicirelli, he says that while elderly vary widely in their attitude and perception of death and the dying process, depending on life experiences and other variables, many do not dread death as we would suppose they might. Many speak of death objectively and appear to view it philosophically. When speaking of the aftereffects of death, some see it as extinction, but most feel there is an afterlife, that death is not the end. When speaking of anticipating death, some see the time remaining as an opportunity to prepare to leave a legacy for the younger generations, either financial or a record of their character and wisdom concerning a good life.

If you remember my discussion of Erik Erikson's stages of human development in Chapter 7, he proposed that in the later part of life there is the tendency of many to engage in generativity, or to want to leave something of value for the younger generation, either wisdom or guidance of some kind, or perhaps something of material value. Cicirelli's study seems to verify that stage.

Some see the prospect of death as a motivator to spur them to accomplish the things they want to accomplish, to do the things left undone. A few of the examples mentioned for using death as a motivator are: to achieve, to be of service, to travel, to spend time with loved ones, and/or to learn new things. Interestingly, when asked whether they would want to live forever if guaranteed good health and adequate financial resources, few said they wanted to live forever. In general, there seems to be little fear of death – some fear perhaps of having pain as death approaches, but not of death itself.

An interesting activity is to compose your own obituary. When I taught a class concerning death and dying, that was one of the student assignments. What would you want people to know about you and remember about you? As in the discussion on attitudes of elderly about dying, perhaps you want to list your accomplishments or the qualities of which you are proud. Perhaps there are little-known facts about your life you'd like to reveal. And perhaps the time to start thinking about that is now.

Thoughts Before I Leave You

I hope by now you have gained insights into the many facets of grief, types of losses, feelings, and behaviors of people in their later years, as well as ways you can work with them and help them enjoy those years. You have gained some knowledge of dementia and how to care for people whose minds are changing and whose memories are fading. Browse the References and Suggested Readings section to see what might interest you in furthering your understanding of aging issues.

Caring for yourself as you go about caring for others is essential and helps you be a better caregiver. Neglecting self-care will affect you and those around you.

Knowing what to expect as death nears can lessen the stress of that caregiving period. The fewer surprises you have, the more easily you can cope.

If you are an elderly person reading this book, you may have realized some grief that you had never labeled as grief, or of which you were unaware, and you may want to talk to someone and lighten your load. Talking about it helps – we're not quite sure *why* it helps, but we know it does.

A final word of heart-felt appreciation to those of you who give care to others – your role is one of the finest, and if you give it your best, you will gain the lasting satisfaction that you made life better for someone in their later years.

Acknowledgements

MANY PEOPLE, BOTH NAMED AND unnamed, both living and deceased, contributed to the bank of knowledge from which I drew my thoughts throughout the writing of this book. My parents, Louise and Darby Anderson; my two husbands – my first, now deceased, Paul T. Johnson, and my current, James (Jim) G. Hanks; my children, Nancy J. Underwood, Mary Catherine (Cathy) Johnson, Paul A. Johnson, and Julie J. Lamb; my brother-in-law, Dr. Richard S. Johnson; my mentor in my profession, as well as in life, Dr. Marythelma Brainard; my editor and mentor in writing, Lois Duncan; those who have experienced much of what this book is about, and who were generous enough to share their experiences; my teacher and professors at The University of Michigan-Dearborn who encouraged me in many ways as an undergraduate, especially Randee Sorscher, Dr. Diane Jones, Dr. John Kotre, Dr. Roger Loeb, Dr. Dan Moerman, and Dr. Dan Swift; my professors in graduate school at The University of New Mexico who supported all my efforts, Dr. David Bachelor, Dr. John Gluck, Dr. Vonda Long, Dr. Joseph Martinez, Dr. Wayne Moellenberg, and Dr. Virginia Shipman; my many clients over the years; my co-workers and the residents at St. Francis Gardens Nursing Home, Manzano del Sol Village, Las Colinas Village Retirement Apartments, and The Woodmark Assisted Living Community; all those who served as readers (and correctors!) of the original manuscript and those who made many valuable suggestions; and a host of others I cannot begin to name, who touched my life in ways they probably do not even realize (like the unknown man who simply smiled at me on my way to class one morning, giving me hope during a dreary time in my life). Never underestimate the value of a smile to a stranger!

References and Suggested Readings

Alway, S.E., Morissette, M.R., & Siu, P.M. (2011). Aging and apoptosis in muscle, in *Handbook of the biology of aging, 7th Edition*, Masoro, E.J. & Austad, S.N. (Eds.) London: Elsevier.

American Psychological Association, *Who are Family Caregivers?* http://www.apa.org/pi/about/publications/caregivers/faq/statistics.aspx

Bain, J. (April, 2015). *Slow fade*, in The Rotarian, Vol. 193(10). Evanston, IL: Rotary International. [Alzheimer's disease]

Barol, J. (Oct. 14, 1999). Allow time, space for grieving after losing a pet, in *The Albuquerque Tribune*, Albuquerque, NM.

Baugher, B., & Jordan, J. (2002). *After suicide loss: Coping with your grief.* Newcastle, WA: Baugher.

Bennett-Goleman, T. (2001). *Emotional alchemy: How the mind can heal the heart.* p. 195. New York: Three Rivers Press.

Birren, J. E. & Deutchman, D. E. (1991). *Guiding autobiography groups for older adults.* Baltimore, MD: Johns Hopkins University Press.

Birren, J. E., & Schaie, K. W. (Eds.) (1996). *Handbook of the psychology of aging, 4th Edition.* San Diego: Academic Press, Inc. [Hearing and Vision]

Boss, P. (2000). *Ambiguous loss: Learning to live with unresolved grief.* Cambridge, MA: Harvard University Press.

Brotman, B. (Feb. 3, 2014). *Eat, drink, be merry and talk about death.* The Chicago Tribune. http://articles.chicagotribune.com/2014-02-03/news/ct-death-dinner-brotman-0203-20140203_1_dinner-conversation-end-of-life-death

Byock, I. (1997). *Dying well: The prospect for growth at the end of life.* New York: Riverhead.

Callone, P. R., Kudlacek, C., Vasiloff, B. C. , Manternach, J., & Brumback, R. A. (2006). *A caregiver's guide to Alzheimer's disease.* New York: Demos Medical Publishing.

Caregiver Action Network, *Caregiving Statistics.* http://caregiveraction.org/statistics/

Carpenter, M. (2013). *Confidence to care: A resource for family caregivers providing Alzheimer's disease or other dementias care at home.* Omaha, NE: Home Instead Press.

Chast, R. (2014). *Can't We Talk About Something More Pleasant?* New York: Bloomsbury.

Chinen, A. B. (1989). *In the ever after: Fairy tales and the second half of life.* Wilmette, IL: Chiron Publications.

Cicirelli, G. C. (2002). *Older adults' views on death.* New York: Springer.

Coberly, L. M., McCormick, J., & Updike, K. (1984). *Writers have no age: Creative writings with older adults, Reprint Edition*. New York: Hawerth Press.

Cole, T. R. (1992). *The journey of life: A cultural history of aging in America.* Cambridge, UK: Cambridge University Press.

Colt, G. H. (1991). *The enigma of suicide.* New York: Simon & Schuster.

Coste, J. K. (2003). *Learning to speak Alzheimer's.* Boston: Houghton Mifflin.

Cousins, N. (1979). *Anatomy of an illness.* New York: W. W. Norton.

Davenport, G.M. (1999). *Working with toxic older adults.* New York: Springer.

Davis, R. (1989). *My journey into Alzheimer's disease.* Carol Stream, IL: Tyndale House.

de Klerk-Rubin, V. (2007). *Validation techniques for dementia care: The family guide to improving communication.* Baltimore: Health Professions Press.

Doka, K. J., (Ed.) with Davidson, J. (1997). *Living with grief when illness is prolonged.* Bristol, PA: Taylor and Francis.

Doka, K. J. (2002). *Living with grief: Loss in later life.* Washington, D.C.: Hospice Foundation of America.

Doka, K. J. (May, 2013). Letter to the editor in *Counseling Today*, published in Alexandria, VA, by The American Counseling Association.

Eckel, S. (Apr., 2015). The ties that unwind, in *Psychology Today*, pp. 74-82. New York, NY: Sussex Publishers.

Edgington, K. (1999). Toast, in *The leap years*, Maier, M.A. & Isom, J.S. (Eds.), pp. 128-131. Boston: Beacon Press.

Erikson, E. H. (1963). *Childhood and society, 2nd Edition.* New York: W.W. Norton.

Eyetech Study Group (April 2002). Preclinical and phase 1a clinical evaluation of an anti-VEGF peg the treatment of exudative age-related macular degeneration, in *Retina: The Journal of Retinal and Vitreous Diseases*, Vol. 22(2), pp. 143-152. http://journals.lww.com/retinajournal/Abstract/2002/04000/Preclinical_and_Phase_1A_Clinical_Evaluation_of_An.2.aspx

Feil, N. (1993). *The validation breakthrough: Simple techniques for communicating with people with "Alzheimer's-type dementia."* Baltimore: Health Professions Press.

Finkelstein, R. (Jan. 2, 2005). Transcending Sorrow, sermon. http://www.rosemike.net/religion/serm_ess/roberta/transorr.html

Florido, R., Tchkonia, T., & Kirklad, J.L. (2011). Aging and adipose tissue, in *Handbook of the biology of aging, 7th Edition*, Masoro, E. J., & Austad, S.N. (Eds.). London: Elsevier.

Foge, L., & Mosconi, G. (2003). *The third choice: A woman's guide to placing a child for adoption, 2nd Edition.* Oakland: Solstice Press.

Fonseca, F. (July 8, 2014). *Grand Canyon, a game-changer in air travel.* http://www.aol.com/article/2014/07/08/grand-canyon-a-game-changer-in-air-travel/20927048/?ncid=webmail1.

Frost, A. (May 14, 2014). *How People Face the Challenges of Caregiving.* Oregon Public Radio Broadcast. http://www.opb.org/radio/programs/thinkoutloud/segment/how-people-face-the-challenges-of-caregiving/

Goldsmith, S. B. (1990). *Choosing a nursing home.* New York: Prentice Hall.

Goyer, A. (Nov., 2013). A crisis around every corner, in *AARP Bulletin.* Washington, D.C.: AARP

Hall, G. S. (published anonymously) (Jan.,1921). Old age, in *The Atlantic Monthly.* Washington, D.C.: Atlantic Media Company.

Halperin, J. (1999). Some bit of love to chew on, in *The leap years*, Maier, M.A. & Isom, J.S., (Eds.), pp. 19-25. Boston: Beacon Press.

Harden, MJ [sic] (1999). *Voices of wisdom: Hawaiian elders speak.* Kula, HI: Aka Press.

Harris, T.A. (2004). *I'm ok – you're ok.* New York: Harper Collins.

Hayflick, L. (1994). *How and why we age.* New York: Ballantine Books.

Hegeleg, A. (Mar. 15, 2014). http://www.thedailybeast.com/articles/2014/03/15/the-flight-370-paradox-how-do-you-mourn-a-missing-person.html

Hogan, B. (June, 2013). *AARP Bulletin*, Vol. 54(5), Talking baseball to beat Alzheimer's. Washington, D.C.: AARP Publications.

Hsu, C., & Sliwa, J.A. (Aug., 2004). Phantom breast pain as a source of functional loss, in *American Journal of Physical Medical Rehabilitation.* 83(8), pp. 659-692.

Hudson, H. (2011). *Kissing tomatoes.* Amazon Digital Services, Inc.: Helen Hudson.

Ilardo, J.A. (1998). *As parents age.* Acton, MA: VanderWyk & Burnham.

Irish, D.P., Lundquist, K.F., & Nelsen, V.J., (Eds.) (1993). *Ethnic variations in dying, death, and grief.* Washington, D.C.: Taylor & Francis.

Isom, J.S. (1999). The night ahead, in *The leap years,* Maier, M.A. & Isom, J.S. (Eds.), pp. 34-37. Boston: Beacon Press.

Jabr, F. (Oct. 15, 2013). Why your brain needs more downtime. In *Scientific American.* http://www.scientificamerican.com/article.dfm?id=mental-downtime

Jaret, P. (March, 2015). An end to blindness? in *AARP Bulletin.* Washington, D.C.: AARP.

Johnson, M.A. (1994). *Writing one's life story: The effects on life satisfaction, cognitive performance, and anxiety related to cognitive performance among women in late adulthood.* Unpublished doctoral dissertation: The University of New Mexico.

Kaminsky, M. (Ed.) (1984). The uses of reminiscence: New ways of working with older adults in *Journal of Gerontological Social Work,* Vol. 7(1/2). New York: Hawerth Press.

Kastenbaum, R.J. (2001). *Death, society, and human experience, 7th Edition.* Boston: Allyn and Bacon.

Kessler, L. (2007). *Finding life in the land of Alzheimer's.* New York: Penguin Books.

Krementz, J. (1982). *How it feels when a parent dies.* New York: Alfred A. Knopf.

Kubler-Ross, E. (1986). *Death: The final stage of growth.* New York: Simon & Schuster.

Kuhn, D. (2003). *Alzheimer's early stages, 2nd Edition.* Alameda, CA: Hunter House.

Langer, E.J. (2009). *Counter clockwise: Mindful health and the power of possibility.* New York: Ballantine Books.

Langer, E.J., & Rodin, J. (1976). The effects of choice and enhanced personal responsibility for the aged: A field experiment in an institutional setting, in *Journal of Personality and Social Psychology*, Vol. 34(2), pp. 191-198.

L'Engle, M. (1999). Ousia: The realness of things, in *The leap years*, Maier, M.A. & Isom, J.S. (Eds.), pp. 38-42. Boston: Beacon Press.

Levine, S. (1982). *Who dies?* New York: Doubleday.

Lynn, J., Harrold, J., & Schuster, J.L. (2011). *Handbook for mortals, 2nd Edition.* New York: Oxford.

McCall, J.B. (1999). *Grief education for caregivers of the elderly.* New York: The Haworth Pastoral Press.

Maclay, E. (1990). *Green winter: Celebrations of later life.* New York: Henry Holt and Company.

Maier, M.A., & Isom, J.S. (Eds.) (1999). *The leap years.* Boston: Beacon Press.

Malgesini, T. (Sept. 28-29, 2013). A group that plays together, stays together. In *East Oregonion Lifestyles*, pg. 1C. Pendleton, OR: East Oregonian Publishing Co.

Marshall, H. (May, 2013). Take years off your looks – instantly! In *Spry*, p. 8, Franklin, TN: PGoA Media.

Martz, S., (Ed.) (1987). *When I am an old woman I shall wear purple.* Manhattan Beach, CA: Papier-Maché Press.

http://www.mayoclinic.com/health/stress-relief/SR00034

Mungo, R. (1994). *Your autobiography.* New York: McMillan.

Musland, H.L. (1992). *The psychotherapy of the elderly self.* New York: Brunner/Mazel.

Neuman, W. (June 2, 2011). Nutrition plate unveiled, replacing food pyramid. Retrieved from http://www.nytimes.com/2011/06/03/business/03plate.html

Nuland, S.B. (1994). *How we die: Reflections on life's final chapter.* New York: Alfred A. Knoff, Inc.

Palmer, G. (1993). *Death: The trip of a lifetime.* San Francisco: Harper.

Piehler, J. M. (February 1, 2014).

http://www.nytimes.com/2014/02/02/opinion/sunday/ashes-to-ashes-but-first-a-nice-pine-box.html

Rodin, J., & Langer, E.J. (1977). Long-term effects of a control-relevant intervention with the institutionalized aged, in *Journal of Personality and Social Psychology*, Vol. 35(12), pp. 879-902.

Rosegrant, S. (Jan. 30, 2014). http://michigantoday.umich.edu/aging-successfully/

Saxon, S.V., Etten, M.J., & Perkins, E.A. (2010). *Physical change & aging, 5th Edition.* New York: Springer Publishing Company.

St. Lifer, H. (April-May, 2013). Hear Today, Gone Tomorrow, in *AARP the magazine.* Washington, D.C.: AARP.

Schneidman, E. (1980). *Voices of death.* Toronto: Bantam.

Schoen, A.M. (2001). *Kindred spirits.* New York: Broadway Books.

Scott-Maxwell, F. (1968). *The measure of my days.* New York: Penguin Books.

Simon, N. (May, 2013) Eye openers, in *AARP Bulletin*, Vol. 54(4). Washington, D.C.: AARP Publications.

Simpson, C. (1996). *At the heart of Alzheimer's, 2nd Edition.* Gaithersburg, MD: Manor Healthcare Corp.

Singh, K.D. (2000). *The grace in dying: How we are transformed spiritually as we die.* http://graceindying.wordpress.com/lesson-3-the-psycho-spiritual-stages-of-dying-and-the-nearing-death-experience/

Sneed, A. (June 2, 2013). http://www.scientificamerican.com/article/studies-link-ddt-other-environmental-toxins-to-late-onset-alzheimers-disease/?print=trueStabler, D. Beating the clock: Tips to stay active as we age, in *The Sunday Oregonian.* Portland, OR.

Speyrer, J.A. (1955). A review of an article by Wilder Penfield, M.D., published in *The Journal of Mental Science* in issue 424, July, 1955, entitled, The Role of the Temporal Cortex in Certain Psychical Phenomena. http://www.primal-page.com/penfield.htm

Stuart-Hamilton, I. (2012). *The psychology of ageing, 5th Edition*. London: Jessica Kingsley.

Sukel, K. (March, 2015). Fostering independence, in *Monitor on Psychology*. Washington, D.C.: American Psychological Association. [Dementia care]

Theroux, P. (Ed.) (1997). *The book of eulogies*. New York: Scribner.

Toseland, R.W. (1995). *Group work with the elderly and family caregivers*. New York: Springer Publishing Co.

Trapasso, B. (June 9, 2013). Public radio presentation: Death café Los Angeles. http://betsytrapasso.com/deathcafelosangeles

Vani, S.D., & Cabrol, P.M. (2012). *Alzheimer's disease: A caregiver's guide*. North Charleston, SC: CreateSpace.

Vincent, G.K. & Velkoff, V.A. (May, 2010). The next four decades: The older population in the United States, 2010 to 2050. http://www.aoa.gov/Aging_Statistics/future_growth/DOCS/p25-1138.pdf

Viney, L.L. (1993). *Life stories: Personal construct therapy with the elderly*. Chichester, England: John Wiley & Sons.

Viorst, J. (1986). *Necessary losses*. New York: Free Press.

Wass, H., Berardo, F.M., & Neimeyer, R.A. (Eds.) (1987). *Dying: Facing the facts, 2nd Edition*. New York: Hemisphere Publishing Corporation.

Wickert, K. M., Dresden, D. S., & Rumrill, Jr., P. D. (2013). *The sandwich generation's guide to eldercare.* New York: DemosHealth.

Wiklund, P. (2000). *Taking charge when you're not in control.* New York: Ballantine Books.

Wilkins, R. (1990). *Death: A history of man's obsessions and fears.* New York: Barnes & Noble.

Williams, M., & Penman, D. (2011). *Mindfulness: An eight-week plan for finding peace in a frantic world.* New York: Rodale.

Wolfelt, A. D., & Duvall, K. J. (2012). *Healing your grief about aging.* Fort Collins, CO: Companion Press.

Wolfelt, A. D., & Duvall, K. J. (2011). *Healing your grieving heart when someone you care about has Alzheimer's.* Fort Collins, CO: Companion Press.

Wood, J. (2013). Adult day services for dementia patients help relieve caregivers' stress. *Psych Central.* Retrieved on June 4, 2013, from http://psychcentral.com/news/2013/05/26/adult-day-services-for-dementia-patients-help-relieve-caregivers-stress/55267.html

Young, H. M., & de Tornyay, R. (1995). *Choices: Making a good move to a retirement community.* Thorofare, NJ: Slack, Inc.

Zarit, S.H., & Knight, B.G. (1996). *A guide to psychotherapy and aging.* Washington, DC: American Psychological Association.

About the Author

Mary A. Johnson received her B.A. in Psychology from The University of Michigan-Dearborn, her M.A. in Family Studies and her Ph.D. in Psychological Foundations of Education with a minor in Aging Studies from The University of New Mexico. While in graduate school she worked in nursing homes in several capacities, took hospice training, obtained a nursing home administrator's license, and after graduation, besides maintaining her private practice, managed a retirement apartment community and two assisted living communities.

She has published in magazines, newspapers, and academic journals, and presented at local, regional, and national conferences and workshops. Her professional memberships include American Counseling Association, American Psychological Association, Association for Death Education and Counseling, New Mexico Psychoanalytic Society, Oregon Counseling Association, and a lifetime membership in Psi Chi International Honor Society in Psychology. She is licensed as a counselor in both New Mexico (LPCC) and Oregon (LPC), and currently is in private practice in Pendleton, Oregon.

You may contact her by email at **MARYABQ@aol.com,** or on her Facebook page, **Mary A. Johnson, Ph.D. Counseling Services**, and she welcomes your inquiries and comments.

45897712R00104

Made in the USA
San Bernardino, CA
24 February 2017